New

THE DEFINITIVE
Hymn
COLLECTION
WITHDRAWN
218 Multi-Denominational Hymns

ISBN 0-634-03354-9

HAL•LEONARD® CORPORATION
7777 W. BLUEMOUND RD. P.O. BOX 13819 MILWAUKEE, WI 53213

Visit Hal Leonard Online at
www.halleonard.com

THE DEFINITIVE Hymn COLLECTION

ABIDE WITH ME

Words by HENRY F. LYTE
Music by WILLIAM H. MONK

A - bide with me. Fast falls the e - ven - tide.
I need Thy pre - sence ev - 'ry pass - ing hour.

The dark - ness deep - ens, Lord, with me a - bide.
What but thy grace can foil the tempt - er's pow'r?

When oth - er help - ers fail and com - forts flee, Help of the
Who, like Thy - self, my guide and stay can be? Through cloud and

ALAS, AND DID MY SAVIOR BLEED

Words by ISAAC WATTS
Music by HUGH WILSON

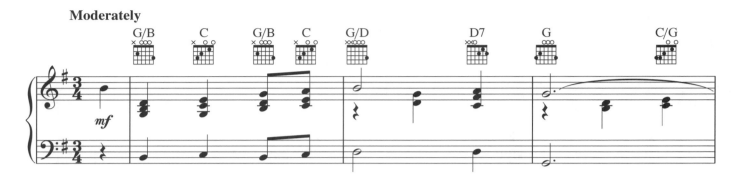

ALL CREATURES OF OUR GOD AND KING

Words by FRANCIS OF ASSISI
Translated by WILLIAM HENRY DRAPER
Music from *Geistliche Kirchengesäng*

ALL GLORY, LAUD AND HONOR

Words by THEODULPH OF ORLEANS
Translated by JOHN MASON NEALE
Music by MELCHIOR TESCHNER
Arranged by WILLIAM HENRY MONK

With dignity

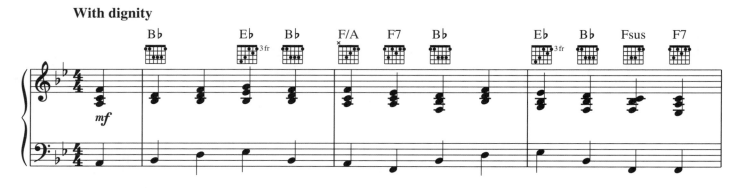

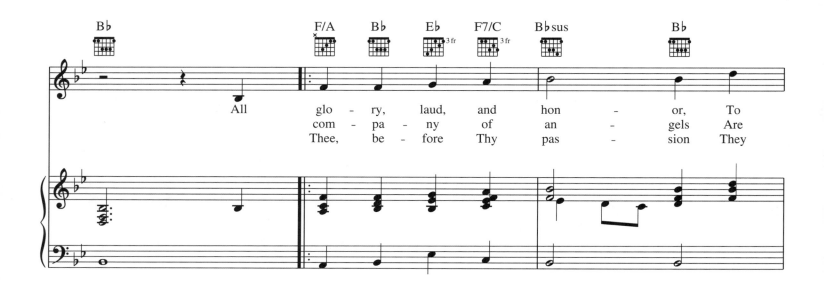

All glo - ry, laud, and hon - or, To
com - pa - ny of an - gels Are
Thee, be - fore Thy pas - sion They

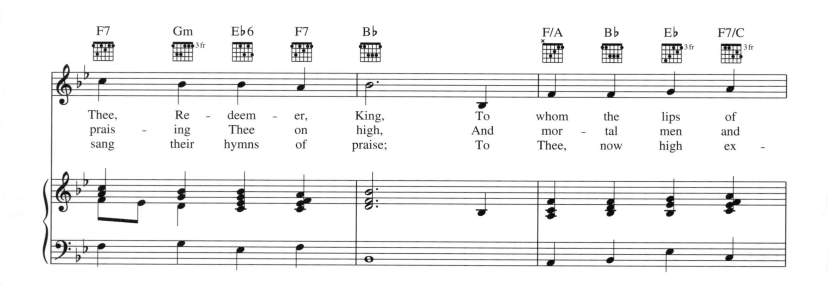

Thee, Re - deem - er, King, To whom the lips of
prais - ing Thee on high, And mor - tal men and
sang their hymns of praise; To Thee, now high ex -

ALL HAIL THE POWER
OF JESUS' NAME

Words by EDWARD PERRONET
Altered by JOHN RIPPON
Music by OLIVER HOLDEN

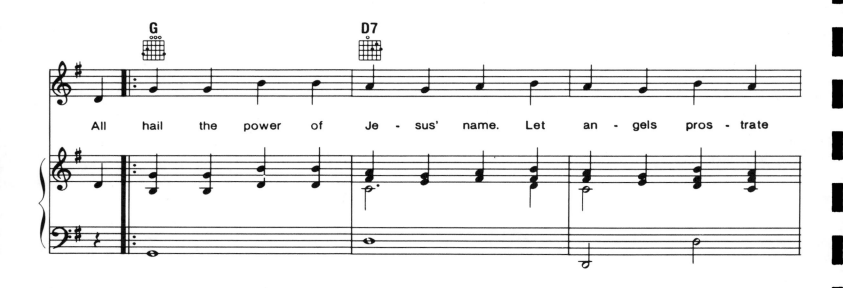

All hail the power of Je - sus' name. Let an - gels pros - trate

fall. Bring forth the roy - al di - a - dem and

2. Let ev'ry kindred, ev'ry tribe on this terrestrial ball.
   To Him all majesty ascribe and crown Him Lord of all.
   To Him all majesty ascribe and crown Him Lord of all.

3. Oh, that with yonder sacred throng we at his feet may fall.
   We'll join the everlasting song and crown Him Lord of all.
   We'll join the everlasting song and crown Him Lord of all.

ALL MY TRIALS

African-American Spiritual

Repeat and Fade

ALL THE WAY MY SAVIOR LEADS ME

Words by FANNY J. CROSBY
Music by ROBERT LOWRY

19

ALL THINGS BRIGHT AND BEAUTIFUL

Words by CECIL FRANCES ALEXANDER
17th Century English Melody
Arranged by MARTIN SHAW

AM I A SOLDIER OF THE CROSS

Words by ISAAC WATTS
Music by THOMAS A. ARNE

AMAZING GRACE

Words by JOHN NEWTON
Traditional American Melody

AND CAN IT BE
THAT I SHOULD GAIN

Words by CHARLES WESLEY
Music by THOMAS CAMPBELL

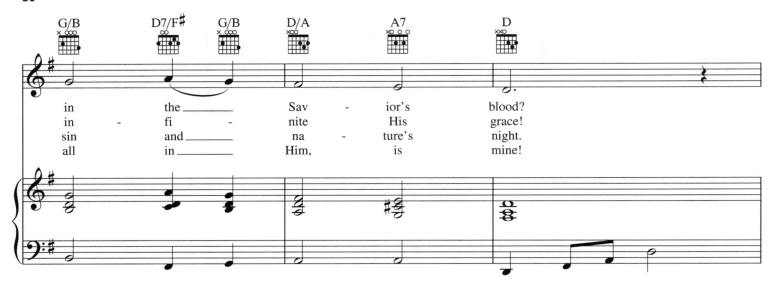

in the _____ Sav - ior's blood?
in - fi - nite His grace!
sin and _____ na - ture's night.
all in _____ Him, is mine!

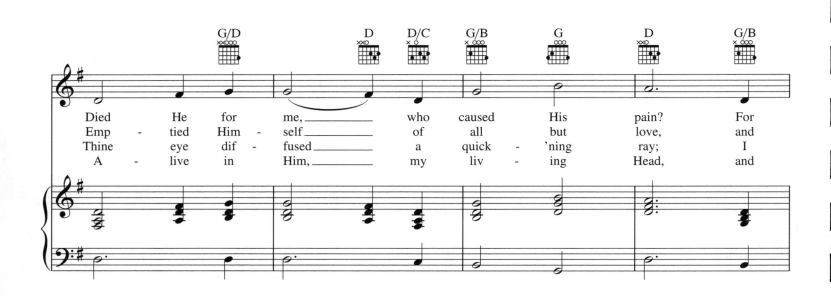

Died He for me, _____ who caused His pain? For
Emp - tied Him - self _____ of all but love, and
Thine eye dif - fused _____ a quick - 'ning ray; I
A - live in Him, _____ my liv - ing Head, and

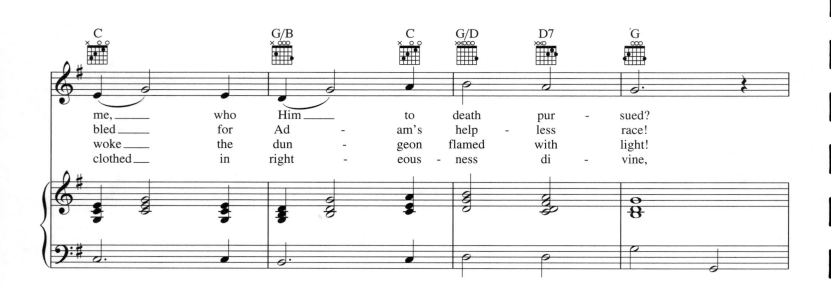

me, _____ who Him _____ to death pur - sued?
bled _____ for Ad - am's help - less race!
woke _____ the dun - geon flamed with light!
clothed _____ in right - eous - ness di - vine,

AMERICA, THE BEAUTIFUL

Words by KATHERINE LEE BATES
Music by SAMUEL A. WARD

1. O beau - ti - ful for spa - cious skies, for am - ber waves of
2. beau - ti - ful for pil - grim feet, whose stern, im - pas - sioned
3., 4. *(See additional verses)*

grain, for pur - ple moun - tain maj - es - ties a - bove the fruit - ed
stress, a thor - ough - fare for free - dom beat a - cross the wil - der -

plain! A - mer - i - ca! A - mer - i - ca! God shed His grace on
ness! A - mer - i - ca! A - mer - i - ca! God mend thine ev - ery

Additional Verses

3. O beautiful for heroes proved
   In liberating strife,
   Who more than self their country loved
   And mercy more than life!
   America! America!
   May God thy gold refine
   'Til all success be nobleness
   And every gain divine.

4. O beautiful for patriot dream
   That sees beyond the years;
   Thine alabaster cities gleam
   Undimmed by human tears.
   America! America!
   God shed His grace on thee,
   And crown thy good with brotherhood,
   From sea to shining sea.

ARE YOU WASHED IN THE BLOOD?

Words and Music by
ELISHA A. HOFFMAN

1. Have you been to Je - sus for the cleans - ing pow'r? Are you
2.-4. *(See additional verses)*

washed in the blood of the Lamb? Are you ful - ly trust-ing in His

grace this hour? Are you washed in the blood of the Lamb? Are you

Refrain

Additional Verses

2. Are you walking daily by the Savior's side?
   Are you washed in the blood of the Lamb?
   Do you rest each moment in the Crucified?
   Are you washed in the blood of the Lamb?
   Refrain

3. When the Bridegroom cometh will your robes be white?
   Are you washed in the blood of the Lamb?
   Will your soul be ready for the mansions bright,
   And be washed in the blood of the Lamb?
   Refrain

4. Lay aside the garments that are stained with sin,
   And be washed in the blood of the Lamb;
   There's a fountain flowing for the soul unclean,
   O be washed in the blood of the Lamb!
   Refrain

ASK YE WHAT GREAT THING I KNOW

Words by JOHANN C. SCHWEDLER
Music by H.A. CÉSAR MALAN

BE PRESENT AT OUR TABLE, LORD

Words by JOHN CENNICK
Music Attributed to LOUIS BOURGEOIS

Be pres-ent at our ta-ble, Lord; be
thank Thee, Lord, for this our food, but

here and ev-'ry-where a-dored. Thy crea-tures bless, and grant that we may
more be-cause of Je-sus' blood. Let man-na to our souls be giv'n, the

feast in Par-a-dise with Thee. We
bread of life sent down from heav'n.

AT CALVARY

Words by WILLIAM R. NEWELL
Music by DANIEL B. TOWNER

1. Years I spent in van - i - ty and pride,
2.-4. *(See additional verses)*

Car - ing not my Lord was cru - ci - fied, Know - ing not it was for

me He died On Cal - va - ry.

Refrain

Mer - cy there was great, and grace was free; Par - don there was mul - ti -

plied to me; There my bur - dened soul found lib - er - ty At

Cal - va - ry. ry.

Additional Verses

2. By God's Word at last my sin I learned;
   Then I trembled at the law I'd spurned,
   Till my guilty soul imploring turned To Calvary.
   Refrain

3. Now I've giv'n to Jesus ev'rything,
   Now I gladly own Him as my King,
   Now my raptured soul can only sing Of Calvary.
   Refrain

4. Oh, the love that drew salvation's plan!
   Oh, the grace that bro't it down to man!
   Oh, the mighty gulf that God did span At Calvary.
   Refrain

AT THE CROSS

Words by ISAAC WATTS and RALPH E. HUDSON
Music by RALPH E. HUDSON

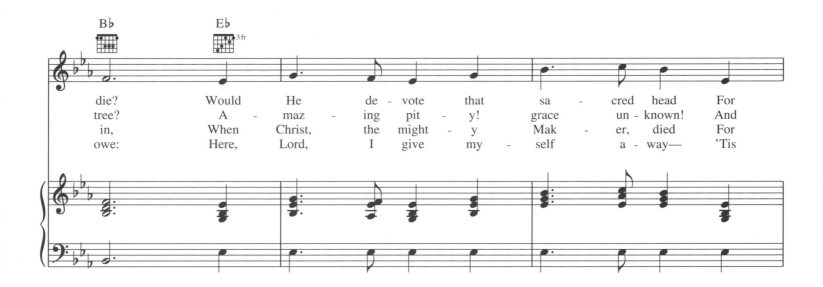

BATTLE HYMN OF THE REPUBLIC

Words by JULIA WARD HOWE
Music by WILLIAM STEFFE

1. Mine eyes have seen the glo - ry of the com - ing of the Lord. He is
2. seen him in the watch-fires of the hun - dred cir - cling camps. They have
3.-5. *(See additional verses)*

tramp - ling out the vin - tage where the grapes of wrath are stored. He hath
build - ed Him an al - tar in the eve - ning dews and damps. I have

loos'd the fate - ful light - ning of His ter - ri - ble swift sword. His
read His right - eous sen - tence by the dim and flar - ing lamps. His

Additional Verses

3. I have read a fiery gospel writ in burnished rows of steel.
As ye deal with my contempters, so with you my grace shall deal.
Let the hero born of woman crush the serpent with his heel,
Since God is marching on.
Refrain

4. He has sounded forth the trumpet that shall never call retreat
He is sifting out the hearts of men before His judgement seat.
O be swift, my soul, to answer Him, be jubilant, my feet.
Our God is marching on.
Refrain

5. In the beauty of the lilies, Christ was born across the sea.
With a glory in His bosom that transfigures you and me.
As He died to make men holy, let us die to make men free,
While God is marching on.
Refrain

BE THOU MY VISION

Traditional Irish
Translated by MARY E. BYRNE

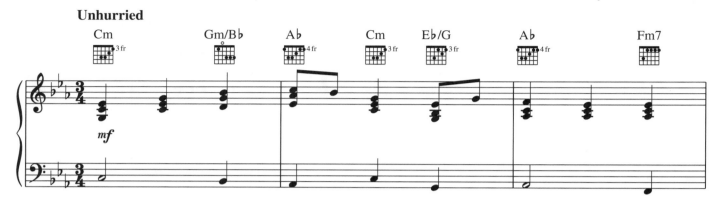

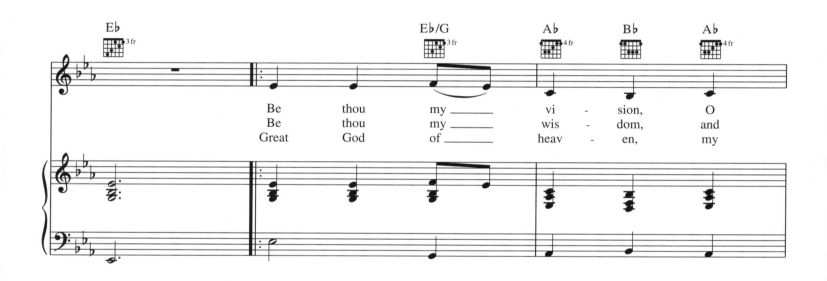

Be thou my _____ vi - sion, O
Be thou my _____ wis - dom, and
Great God of _____ heav - en, my

Lord of my heart; naught be all else to me,
thou my true word; I ev - er with thee and
vic - to - ry won, may I reach heav - en's joys,

BEAUTIFUL ISLE OF SOMEWHERE

Words by JESSIE B. POUNDS
Music by JOHN S. FEARIS

Some - where the sun is shin - ing;
Some - where the day is long - er;
Some - where the load is lift - ed,

some - where the song - birds dwell. _____
some - where the task is done. _____
close by an o - pen gate. _____

Hush then thy sad re -
Some - where the heart is
Some - where the clouds are

BEAUTIFUL SAVIOR

Words from *Munsterisch Gesangbuch*
Translated by JOSEPH A. SEISS
Music adapted from a Silesian Folk Tune

BENEATH THE CROSS OF JESUS

Words by ELIZABETH C. CLEPHANE
Music by FREDERICK C. MAKER

BEULAH LAND

Words by EDGAR PAGE STITES
Music by JOHN R. SWENEY

1. I've reached the land of
2., 3. *(See additional verses)*

love di-vine And all its rich - es free - ly mine; Here shines un-dimmed one

bliss - ful day, For all my night has passed a-way. O Beu - lah Land, sweet

Additional Verses

2. **My Savior comes and walks with me,**
   And sweet communion here have we;
   He gently leads me by His hand,
   For this is heaven's borderland.
   Refrain

3. **The zephyrs seem to float to me,**
   Sweet sounds of heaven's melody,
   As angels with the white-robed throng
   Join in the sweet Redemption song.
   Refrain

BLESSED ASSURANCE

Lyrics by FANNY J. CROSBY
Music by PHOEBE PALMER KNAPP

With movement

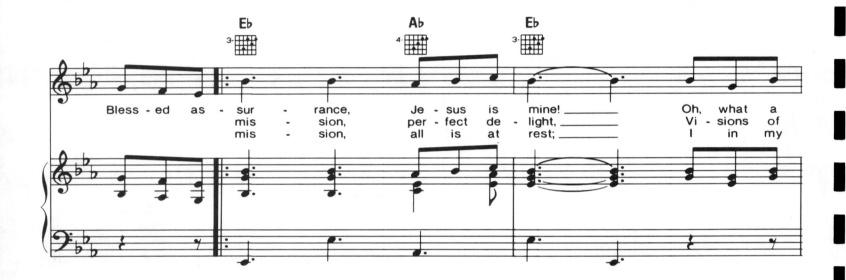

Bless - ed as - sur - rance, Je - sus is mine! _____ Oh, what a
mis - sion, per - fect de - light, _____ Vi - sions of
mis - sion, all is at rest; _____ I in my

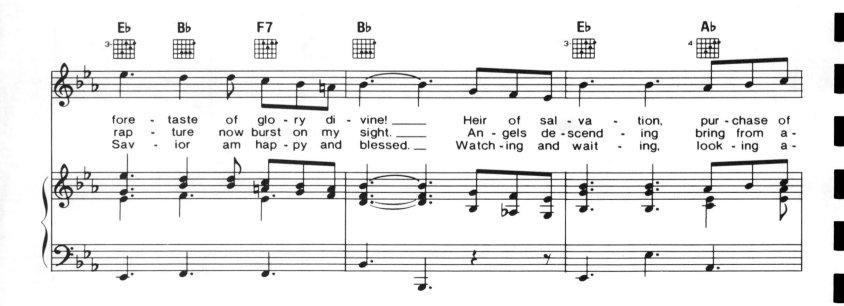

fore - taste of glo - ry di - vine! _____ Heir of sal - va - tion, pur - chase of
rap - ture now burst on my sight. _____ An - gels de - scend - ing bring from a -
Sav - ior am hap - py and blessed. __ Watch - ing and wait - ing, look - ing a -

BLEST BE THE TIE THAT BINDS

Words by JOHN FAWCETT
Music by JOHANN G. NÄGELI
Arranged by LOWELL MASON

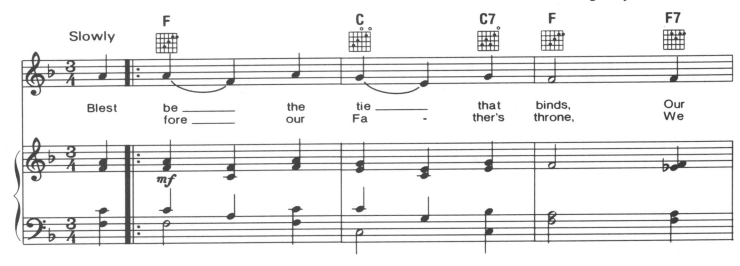

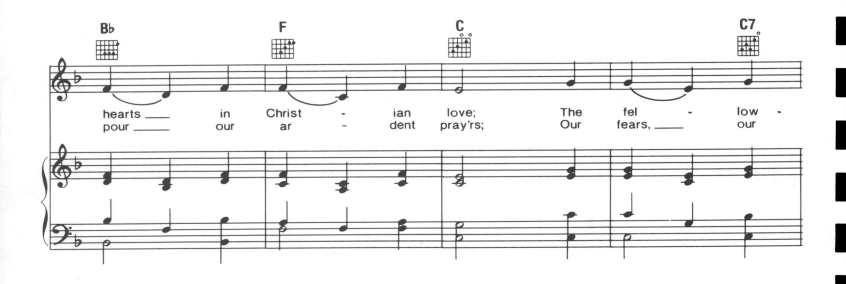

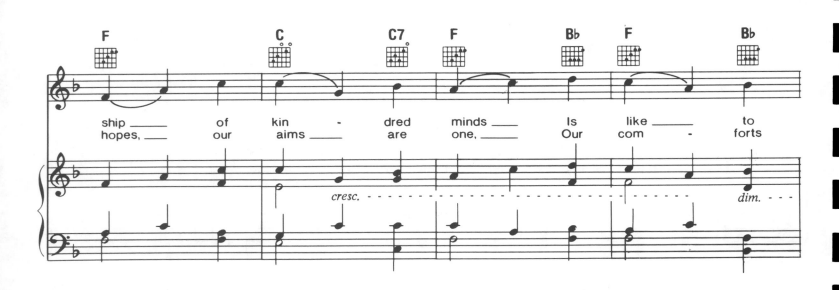

BREAK THOU THE BREAD OF LIFE

Words by MARY ARTEMESIA LATHBURY
Music by WILLIAM FISKE SHERWIN

Reverently

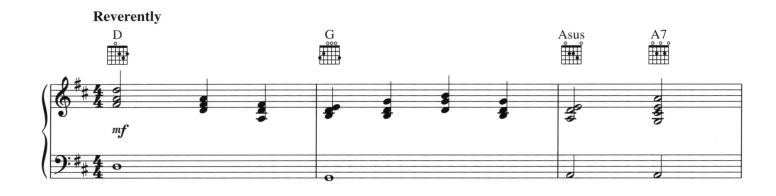

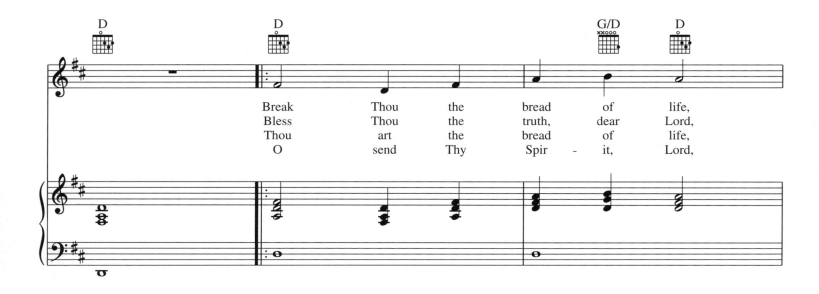

Break Thou the bread of life,
Bless Thou the truth, dear Lord,
Thou art the bread of life,
O send Thy Spir - it, Lord,

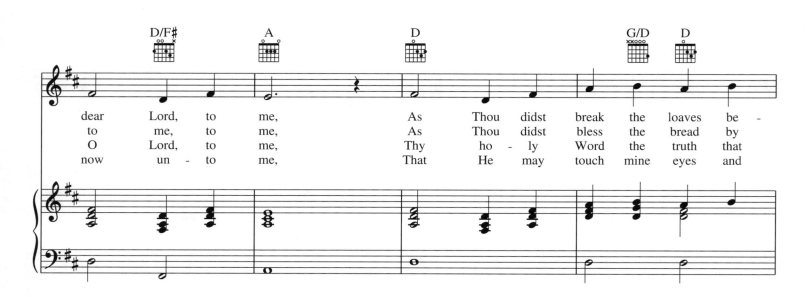

dear Lord, to me, As Thou didst break the loaves be-
to me, to me, As Thou didst bless the bread by
O Lord, to me, Thy ho - ly Word the truth that
now un - to me, That He may touch mine eyes and

BREATHE ON ME, BREATH OF GOD

Words by EDWIN HATCH
Music by ROBERT JACKSON

BRIGHTEN THE CORNER
WHERE YOU ARE

Words by INA DULEY OGDON
Music by CHARLES H. GABRIEL

BRINGING IN THE SHEAVES

Words by KNOWLES SHAW
Music by GEORGE A. MINOR

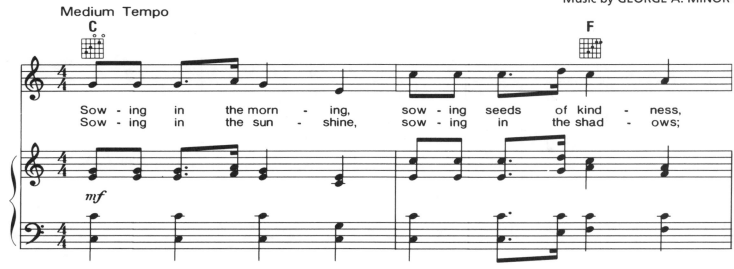

3. Going forth with weeping, sowing for the Master.
   Tho' the loss sustained our spirit often grieves;
   When our weeping's over, He will bid us welcome,
   We shall come rejoicing, bringing in the sheaves.

A CHILD OF THE KING

Words by HARRIET E. BUELL
Music by JOHN B. SUMNER

Moderately, with a lilt

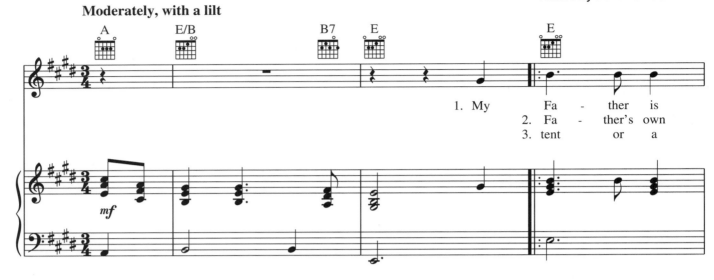

1. My Fa - ther is
2. Fa - ther's own
3. tent or a

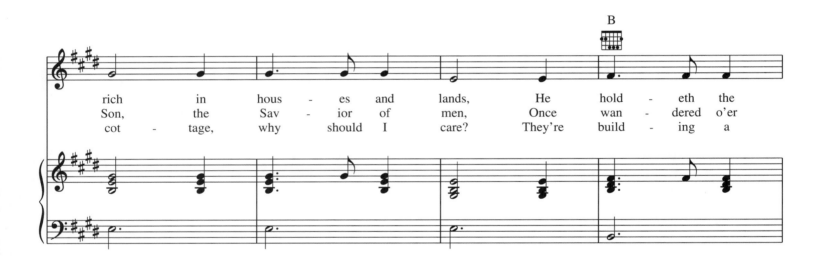

rich in hous - es and lands, He hold - eth the
Son, the Sav - ior of men, Once wan - dered o'er
cot - tage, why should I care? They're build - ing a

wealth of the world in His hands! Of ru - bies and
earth as the poor - est of them; But now He is
pal - ace for me o - ver there! Though here I'm a

CHRIST AROSE
(Low in the Grave He Lay)

Words and Music by
ROBERT LOWRY

Triumphantly

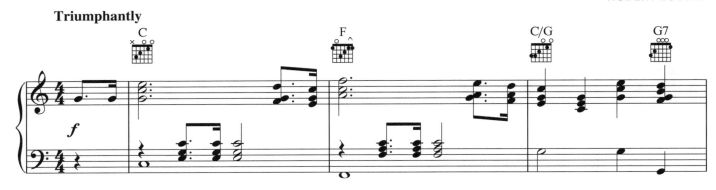

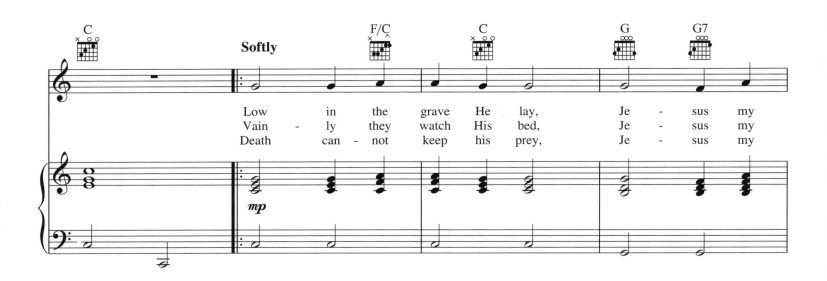

Low in the grave He lay, Je - sus my
Vain - ly they watch His bed, Je - sus my
Death can - not keep his prey, Je - sus my

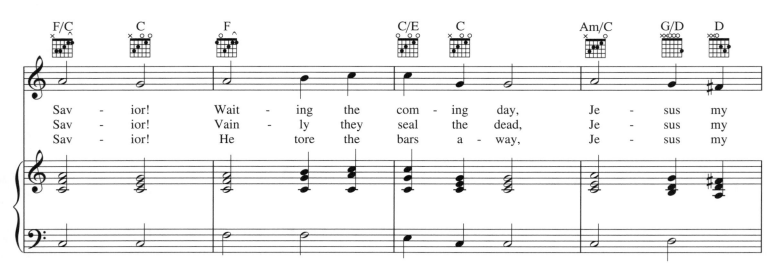

Sav - ior! Wait - ing the com - ing day, Je - sus my
Sav - ior! Vain - ly they seal the dead, Je - sus my
Sav - ior! He tore the bars a - way, Je - sus my

CHRIST THE LORD IS RISEN TODAY

Words by CHARLES WESLEY
Music adapted from *Lyra Davidica*

Additional Verses

2. Lives again our glorious King: Alleluia!
   Where, O death, is now thy sting? Alleluia!
   Dying once, He all doth save: Alleluia!
   Where thy victory, O grave? Alleluia!

3. Love's redeeming work is done, Alleluia!
   Fought the fight, the battle won: Alleluia!
   Death in vain forbids Him rise: Alleluia!
   Christ has opened Paradise. Alleluia!

4. Soar we now, where Christ has led, Alleluia!
   Foll'wing our exalted Head: Alleluia!
   Made like Him, like Him we rise: Alleluia!
   Ours the cross, the grave, the skies. Alleluia!

CHURCH IN THE WILDWOOD

Words and Music by
DR. WILLIAM S. PITTS

There's a church in the val-ley by the wild - wood, no
come to the church _ in the wild - wood, to the
church in the val-ley by the wild - wood, when

love - li - er spot in the dale.   No ___ place is so dear to my
trees where the wild - flow - ers bloom,   where the part - ing ___ hymn will be
day fades a - way in - to night,   I would fain from this spot of my

THE CHURCH'S ONE FOUNDATION

Words by SAMUEL JOHN STONE
Music by SAMUEL SEBASTIAN WESLEY

2. Elect from every nation,
   Yet one o'er all the earth,
   Her charter of salvation,
   One Lord, one faith, one birth;
   One holy name she blesses,
   Partakes one holy food,
   And to one hope she presses,
   With every grace endued.

3. 'Mid toil and tribulation,
   And tumult of her war,
   She waits the consummation
   Of peace for evermore;
   Till with the vision glorious,
   Her longing eyes are blest,
   And the great Church victorious
   Shall be the Church at rest.

4. Yet she on earth hath union
   With God, the Three in One,
   And mystic sweet communion
   With those whose rest is won;
   O happy ones and holy!
   Lord give us grace that we
   Like them, the meek and lowly,
   On high may dwell with Thee.

CLOSE TO THEE

Words by FANNY J. CROSBY
Music by SILAS J. VAIL

COME, THOU ALMIGHTY KING

Anonymous Text
Music by FELICE DE GIARDINI

3. Come, holy Comforter!
   Thy sacred witness bear,
   In this glad hour:
   Thou who almighty art,
   Now rule in ev'ry heart,
   And ne'er from us depart,
   Spirit of pow'r!

4. To the great One in Three,
   The highest praises be,
   Hence ever more!
   His sov'reign majesty
   May we in glory see,
   And to eternity
   Love and adore.

COUNT YOUR BLESSINGS

Words by JOHNSON OATMAN, JR.
Music by EDWIN O. EXCELL

When up-on life's bil-lows you are tem-pest tossed,
Are you ev-er bur-dened with a load of care?
When you look at oth-ers with their lands and gold,
So, a-mid the con-flict, wheth-er great or small,

when you are dis-cour-aged, think-ing all is lost,
Does the cross seem heav-y you are called to bear?
think that Christ has prom-ised you His wealth un-told.
do not be dis-cour-aged; God is o-ver all.

COME, THOU FOUNT OF EVERY BLESSING

Words by ROBERT ROBINSON
Music from John Wyeth's *Repository of Sacred Music*

COME, YE FAITHFUL, RAISE THE STRAIN

Words by JOHN OF DAMASCUS
Translated by JOHN MASON NEALE
Music by ARTHUR SEYMOUR SULLIVAN

Joyfully

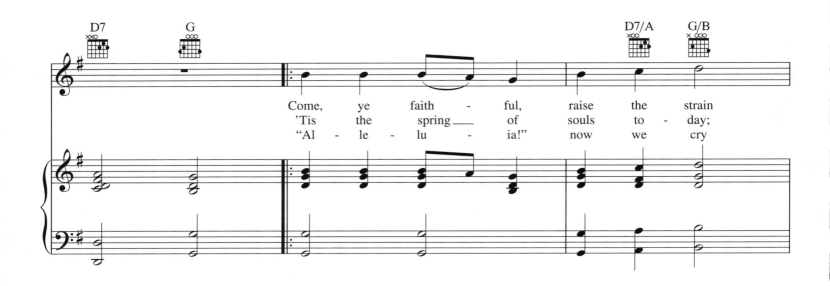

Come, ye faith - ful, raise the strain
'Tis the spring____ of souls to - day;
"Al - le - lu - ia!" now we cry

of tri - um - phant glad - ness! God hath brought____ forth
Christ hath burst His pris - on, and from three____ days'
to our King im - mor - tal, who, tri - um - phant,

COME, YE THANKFUL PEOPLE, COME

Words by HENRY ALFORD
Music by GEORGE JOB ELVEY

Stately

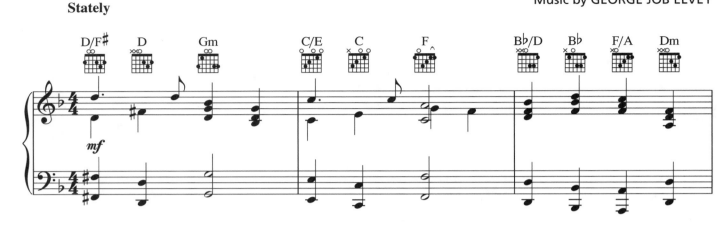

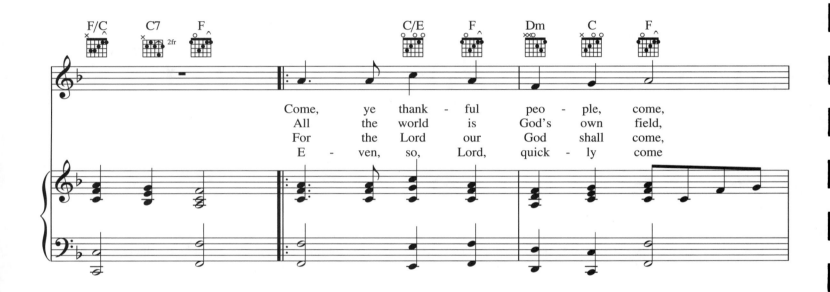

Come, ye thank-ful peo-ple, come,
All ye the world is God's own field,
For the Lord our God shall come,
E-ven, so, Lord, quick-ly come

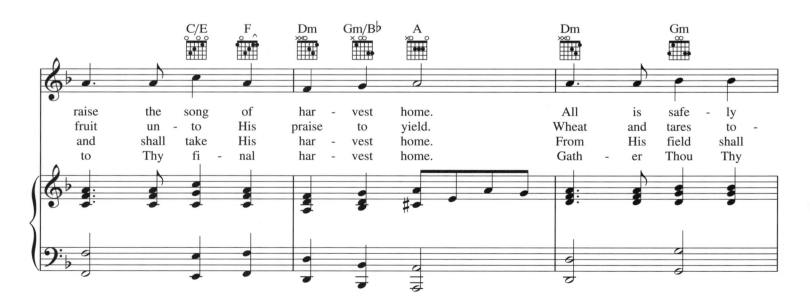

raise the song of har-vest home.
fruit un-to His praise to yield.
and shall take His har-vest home.
to Thy fi-nal har-vest home.

All is safe-ly
Wheat and tares to-
From His field shall
Gath-er Thou Thy

CROWN HIM WITH MANY CROWNS

Words by MATTHEW BRIDGES and GODFREY THRING
Music by GEORGE JOB ELVEY

3. Crown Him the Lord of life, Who triumphed o'er the grave
And rose victorious in the strife for those He came to save.
His glories now we sing, Who dies and rose on high,
Who dies eternal life to bring and lives that death may die.

DAY IS DYING IN THE WEST

Words by MARY A. LATHBURY
Music by WILLIAM F. SHERWIN

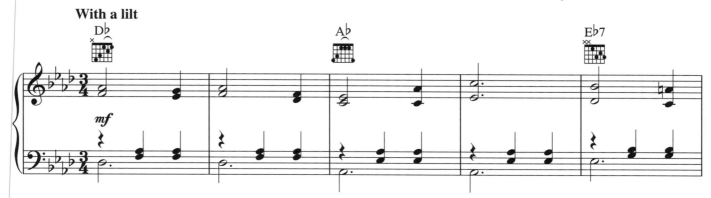

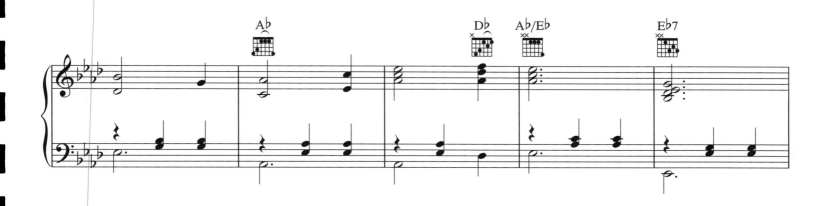

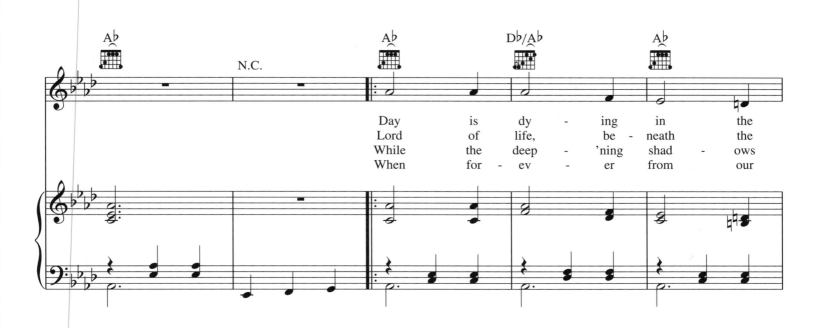

Day is dy - ing in the
Lord of life, be - neath the
While the deep - 'ning shad - ows
When for - ev - er from our

DEAR LORD AND FATHER OF MANKIND

Words by JOHN GREENLEAF WHITTIER
Music by FREDERICK CHARLES MAKER

DOWN BY THE RIVERSIDE

African-American Spiritual

DEEP RIVER

African-American Spiritual
Based on Joshua 3

DOWN AT THE CROSS
(Glory to His Name)

Words by ELISHA A. HOFFMAN
Music by JOHN H. STOCKTON

ETERNAL FATHER, STRONG TO SAVE

Words by WILLIAM WHITING
Music by JOHN BACCHUS DYKES

1. E - ter - nal Fa - ther, strong to save, Whose
2.-4. *(See additional verses)*

arm doth blind the rest - less wave, Who bidd'st the might - y

o - cean deep its own ap - point - ed lim - its keep: O

Additional Verses

2. O Savior, whose almighty word
   The winds and waves submissive heard,
   Who walkedst on the foaming deep
   And calm amid its rage didst sleep:
   O hear us when we cry to Thee
   For those in peril on the sea.

3. O sacred Spirit, who didst brood
   Upon the chaos dark and rude,
   Who bad'st its angry tumult cease,
   And gavest light and life and peace:
   O hear us when we cry to Thee
   For those in peril on the sea.

4. O Trinity of love and power,
   Our brethren shield in danger's hour;
   From rock and tempest, fire and foe,
   Protect them wheresoe'er they go;
   And ever let there rise to Thee
   Glad hymns of praise from land and sea. Amen.

EVERY TIME I FEEL THE SPIRIT

African-American Spiritual

FAIREST LORD JESUS

Words from *Munster Gesangbuch*
Verse 4 by JOSEPH A. SEISS
Music from *Schlesische Volkslieder*
Arranged by RICHARD STORRS WILLIS

Warmly

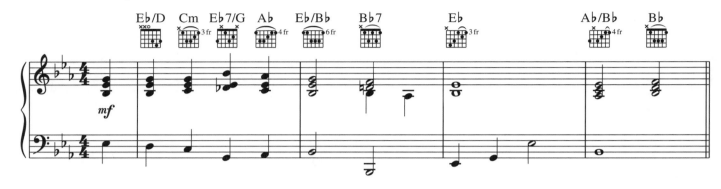

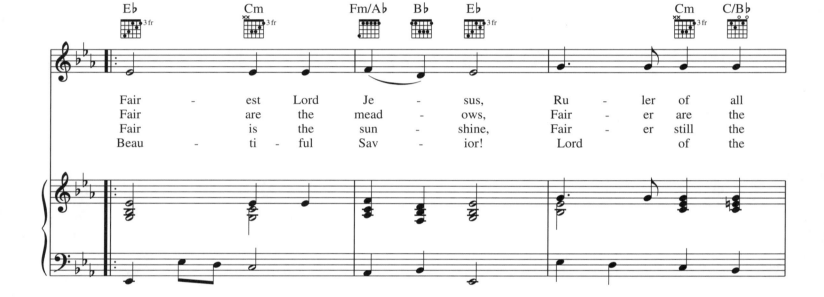

Fair - est Lord Je - sus, Ru - ler of all
Fair are the mead - ows, Fair - er are the
Fair is the sun - shine, Fair - er still the
Beau - ti - ful Sav - ior! Lord of the

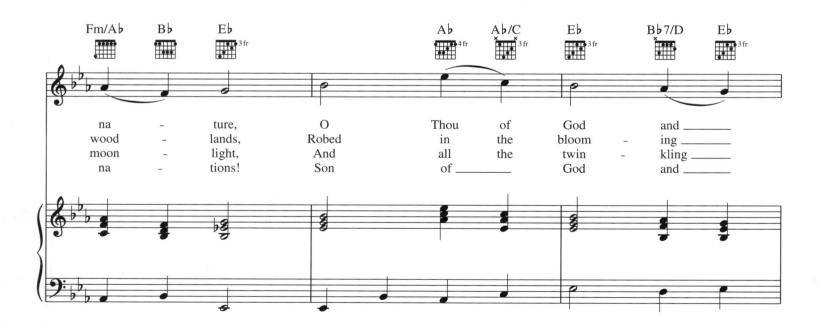

na - ture, O Thou of God and _____
wood - lands, Robed in the bloom - ing _____
moon - light, And all the twin - kling _____
na - tions! Son of _____ God and _____

FAITH OF OUR FATHERS

Words by FREDERICK WILLIAM FABER
Music by HENRI F. HEMY and JAMES G. WALTON

FOOTSTEPS OF JESUS

Words by MARY B.C. SLADE
Music by ASA B. EVERETT

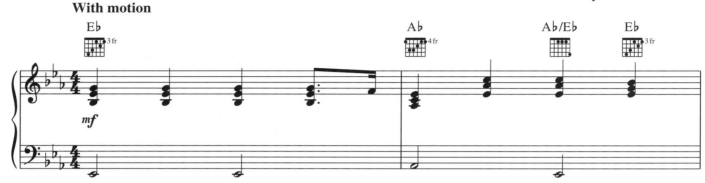

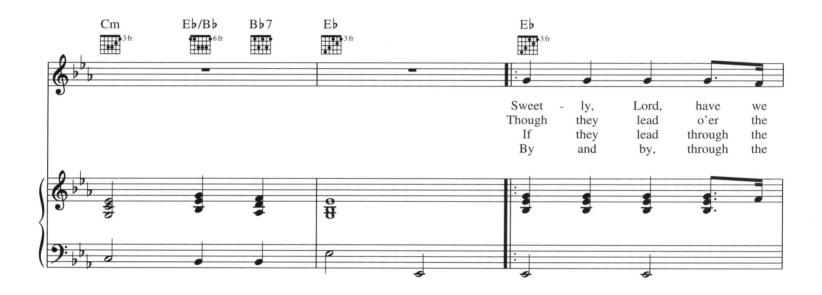

Sweet - ly, Lord, have we heard Thee call - ing, "Come, fol - low Me!"
Though they lead o'er the cold, dark moun - tains, Seek - ing His sheep;
If they lead through the tem - ple ho - ly, Preach - ing the Word;
By and by, through the shin - ing por - tals, Turn - ing our feet,

FOR ALL THE BLESSINGS OF THE YEAR

Words by ALBERT H. HUTCHINSON
Music by ROBERT N. QUAILE

FOR ALL THE SAINTS

Words by WILLIAM W. HOW
Music by RALPH VAUGHAN WILLIAMS

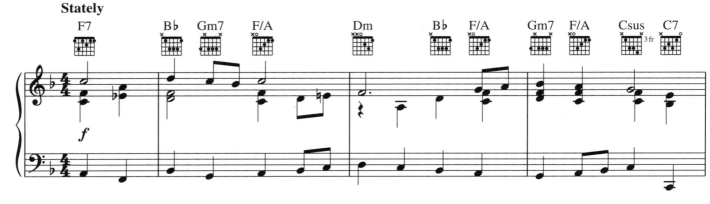

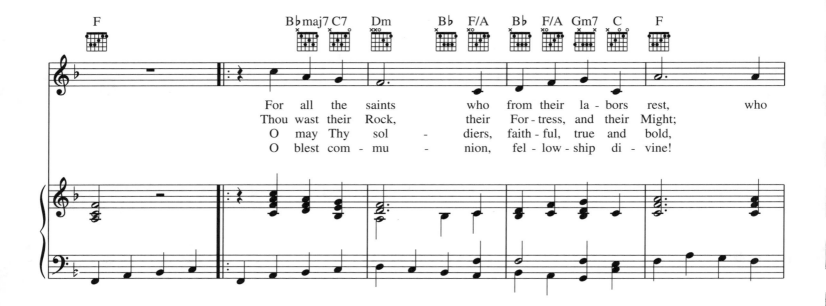

For all the saints who from their la - bors rest, who
Thou wast their Rock, their For - tress, and their Might;
O may Thy sol - diers, faith - ful, true and bold,
O blest com - mu - nion, fel - low - ship di - vine!

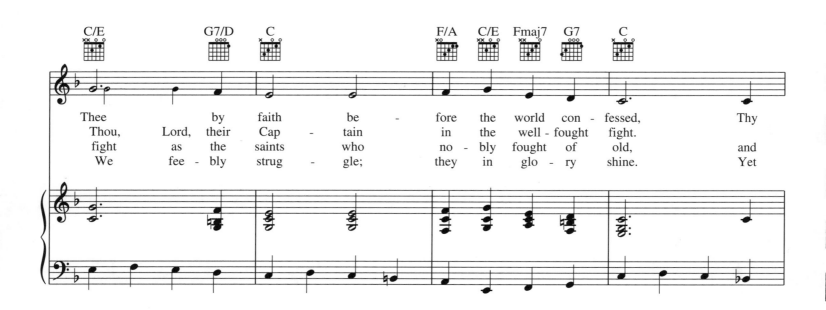

Thee by faith be - fore the world con - fessed, Thy
Thou, Lord, their Cap - tain in the well - fought fight.
fight as the saints who no - bly fought of old, and
We fee - bly strug - gle; they in glo - ry shine. Yet

HE'S GOT THE WHOLE WORLD
IN HIS HANDS

Traditional Spiritual

FOR THE BEAUTY OF THE EARTH

Text by FOLLIOT S. PIERPOINT
Music by CONRAD KOCHER

* for Holy Communion

GIVE ME THAT OLD TIME RELIGION

Traditional

Moderately bright

mf

Chorus

Give Me That Old Time Re - li - gion; Give Me That Old Time Re -

li - gion. Give Me That Old Time Re - li - gion and it's good e - nough for

Verse

me. 1. It was good for the Proph - et Dan - iel; it was
good for Paul and Si - las, it was

3. It was good for old Abe Lincoln;
It was good for old Abe Lincoln.
It was good for old Abe Lincoln,
And it's good enough for me.

GOD BE WITH YOU TILL WE MEET AGAIN

Words by JEREMIAH E. RANKIN
Music by WILLIAM G. TOMER

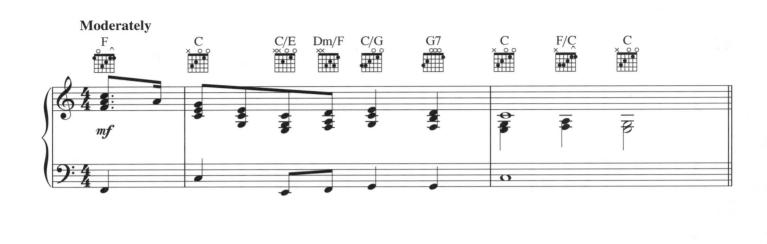

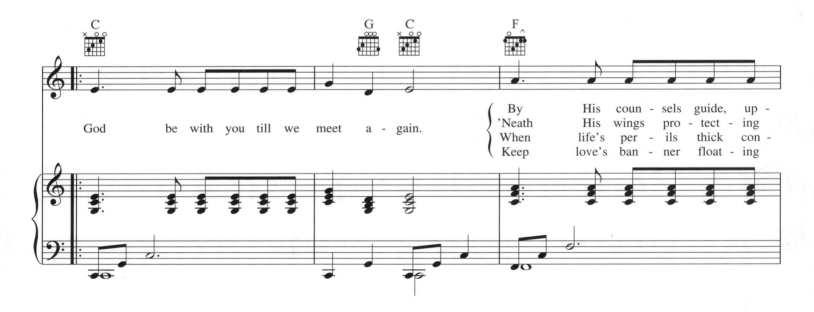

God be with you till we meet a - gain.

By His coun - sels guide, up -
'Neath His wings pro - tec - ting
When life's per - ils thick con -
Keep love's ban - ner float - ing

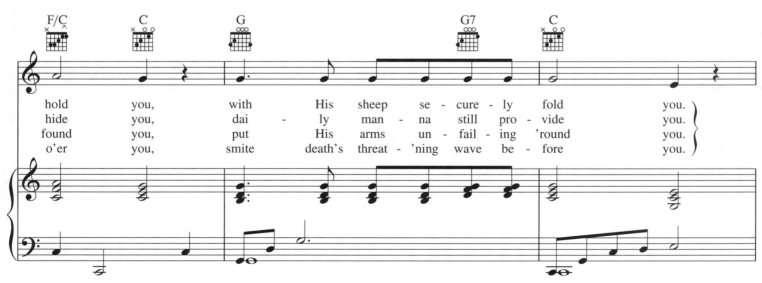

hold you, with His sheep se - cure - ly fold you.
hide you, dai - ly man - na still pro - vide you.
found you, put His arms un - fail - ing 'round you.
o'er you, smite death's threat - 'ning wave be - fore you.

GOD OF OUR FATHERS

Words by DANIEL CRANE ROBERTS
Music by GEORGE WILLIAM WARREN

GOD WILL TAKE CARE OF YOU

Words by CIVILLA D. MARTIN
Music by W. STILLMAN MARTIN

GUIDE ME, O THOU GREAT JEHOVAH

Words by WILLIAM WILLIAMS
Music by JOHN HUGHES

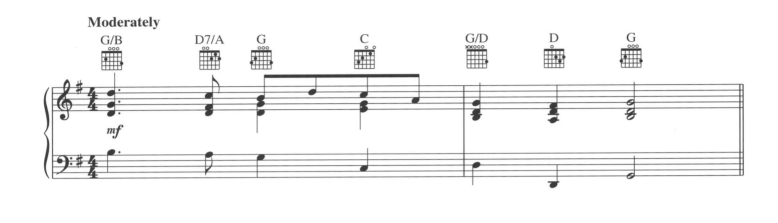

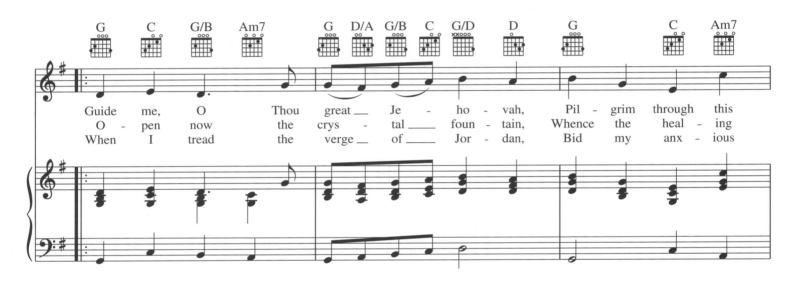

Guide me, O Thou great ___ Je - ho - vah, Pil - grim through this
O - pen now the crys - tal ___ foun - tain, Whence the heal - ing
When I tread the verge ___ of ___ Jor - dan, Bid my anx - ious

bar - ren land. I am weak, but Thou ___ art ___ might - y;
stream doth flow. Let the fire and cloud - y ___ pil - lar
fears sub - side. Bear me through the swell - ing ___ cur - rent,

HAVE THINE OWN WAY, LORD

Words by ADELAIDE A. POLLARD
Music by GEORGE C. STEBBINS

139

HE HIDETH MY SOUL

Words by FANNY J. CROSBY
Music by WILLIAM J. KIRKPATRICK

HE LEADETH ME

Words by JOSEPH H. GILMORE
Music by WILLIAM B. BRADBURY

HEAVENLY SUNLIGHT

Words by HENRY J. ZELLEY
Music by GEORGE HARRISON COOK

HIGHER GROUND

Words by JOHNSON OATMAN, JR.
Music by CHARLES H. GABRIEL

I'm press-ing on the up-ward
I want to live a-bove the
I want to scale the ut-most

way, new heights I'm gain-ing ev-'ry day; still pray-ing
world, tho Sa-tan's darts at me are hurled; still for faith has
height, and catch a gleam of glo-ry bright; but still I'll

HIS EYE IS ON THE SPARROW

Words by CIVILLA D. MARTIN
Music by CHARLES H. GABRIEL

Why should I feel dis-cour-aged? ___ Why should the shad-ows come? ___
"Let not your heart be troub-led," ___ His ten-der word I hear, ___
When-ev-er I am tempt-ed, ___ When-ev-er clouds a-rise, ___

Why should my heart be lone-ly, ___ And long for heav'n and home, ___ When
And rest-ing on His good-ness, ___ I lose my doubts and fears, ___ Tho'
When song gives place to sigh-ing, ___ When hope with-in me dies, ___ I

HOLY GOD, WE PRAISE THY NAME

Words and Music from *Katholisches Gesangbuch*
Words attributed to IGNAZ FRANZ
Translated by CLARENCE WALWORTH

Boldly, With Movement

Ho - ly God, ____ We Praise ____ Thy Name;

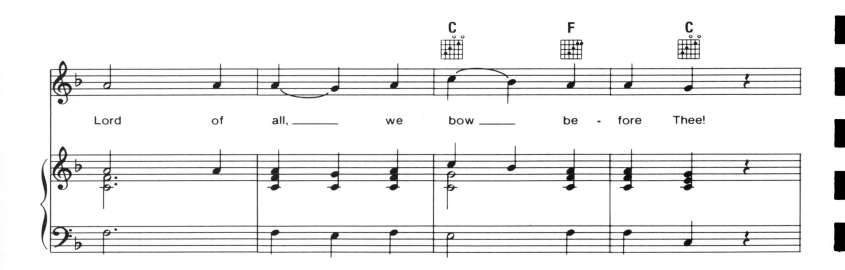

Lord of all, ____ we bow ____ be - fore Thee!

All on earth ____ Thy scep - tre claim, All in

HOLY, HOLY, HOLY

Text by REGINALD HEBER
Music by JOHN B. DYKES

154

HOSANNA, LOUD HOSANNA

Words by JONNETTE THRELFALL,
Based on Matthew 21:1-11
Music from *Gesangbuch der Herzogl*

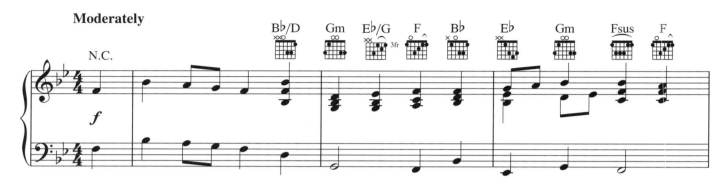

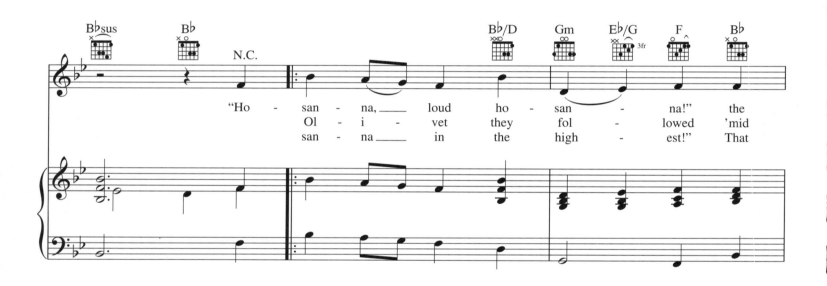

"Ho - san - na,____ loud ho - san ____ na!" the
Ol - i - vet they fol - lowed 'mid
san - na____ in the high - est!" That

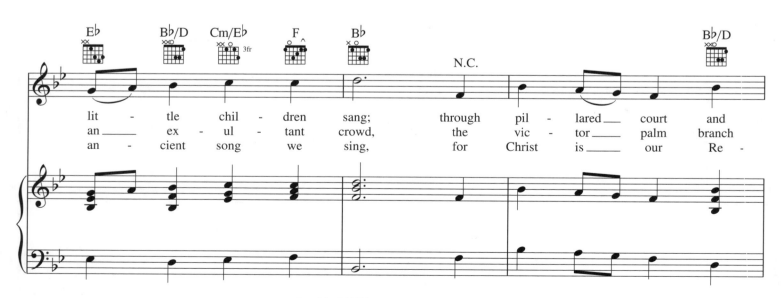

lit - tle chil - dren sang; through pil - lared____ court and
an____ ex - ul - tant crowd, the vic - tor____ palm branch
an - cient song we sing, for Christ is____ our Re -

HOW CAN I KEEP FROM SINGING

American Folk Hymn

HOW FIRM A FOUNDATION

Traditional text compiled by JOHN RIPPON
Traditional music compiled by JOSEPH FUNK

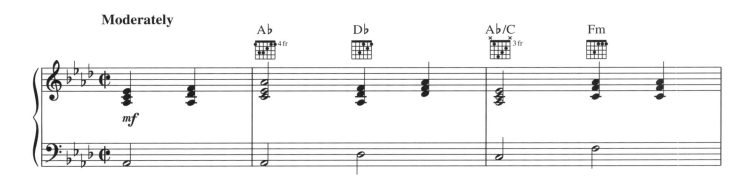

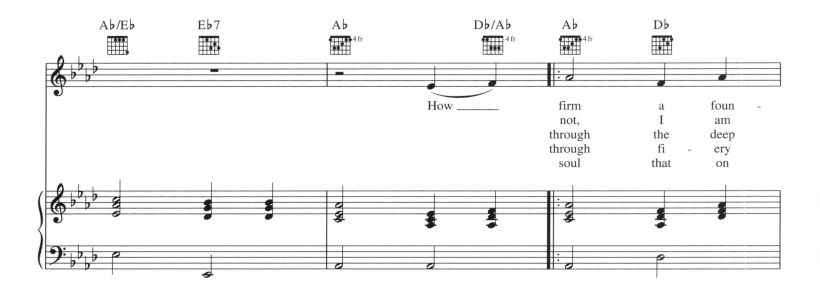

How ___ firm a foun -
not, I am
through the deep
through fi - ery
soul that on

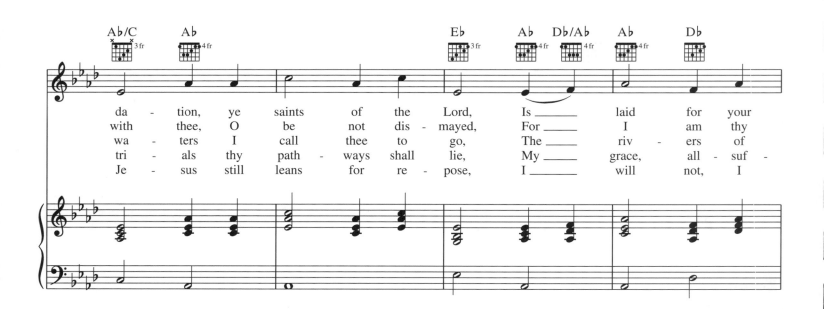

da - tion, ye saints of the Lord, Is ___ laid for your
with thee, O be not dis - mayed, For ___ I am thy
wa - ters I call thee to go, The ___ riv - ers of
tri - als thy path - ways shall lie, My ___ grace, all - suf -
Je - sus still leans for re - pose, I ___ will not, I

HOW SWEET THE NAME OF JESUS SOUNDS

Words by JOHN NEWTON
Music by ALEXANDER REINAGLE

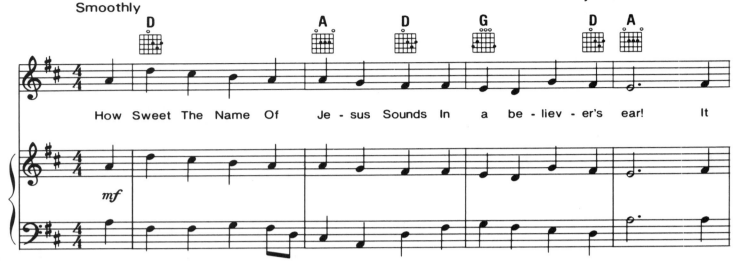

How Sweet The Name Of Je - sus Sounds In a be - liev - er's ear! It

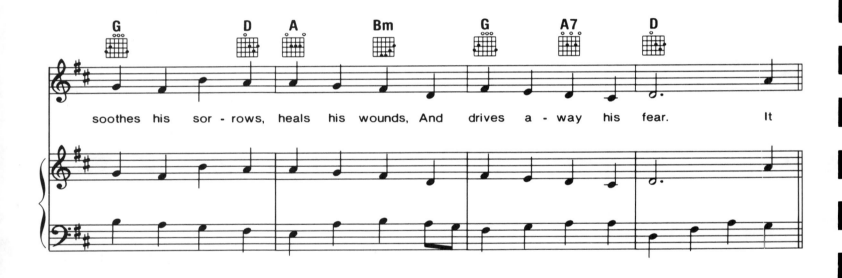

soothes his sor - rows, heals his wounds, And drives a - way his fear. It

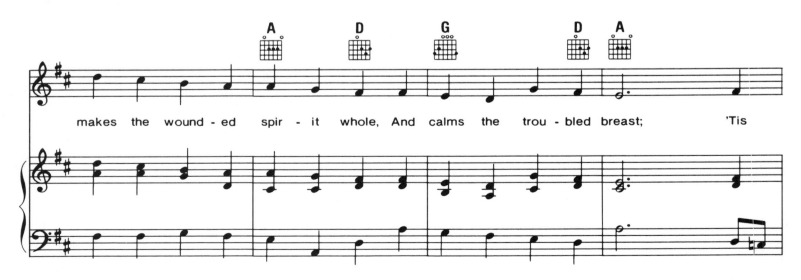

makes the wound - ed spir - it whole, And calms the trou - bled breast; 'Tis

I AM THINE, O LORD

Words by FANNY J. CROSBY
Music by WILLIAM H. DOANE

I am Thine, O Lord, I have heard Thy voice, And it
crate me now to Thy ser - vice, Lord, By the
pure de - light of a sin - gle hour That the be -
depths of love that I can - not know Till I

told Thy love to _____ me; But I long to rise in the
pow'r of grace di - vine; Let my soul look up with a
fore Thy throne I _____ spend, When I kneel in prayer, and with
cross the nar - row _____ sea; There are heights of joy that I

I HAVE DECIDED TO FOLLOW JESUS

Folk Melody from India
Arranged by AUILA READ

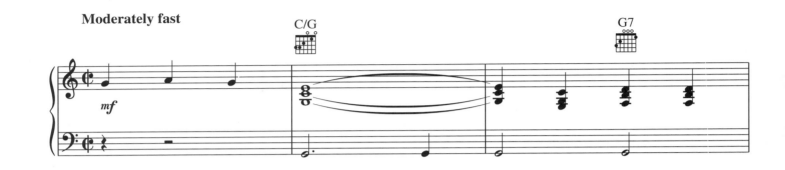

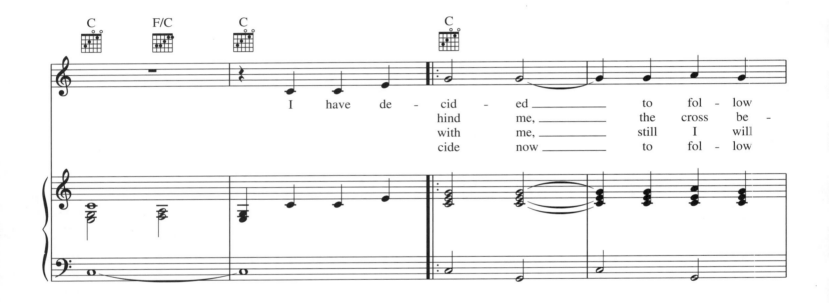

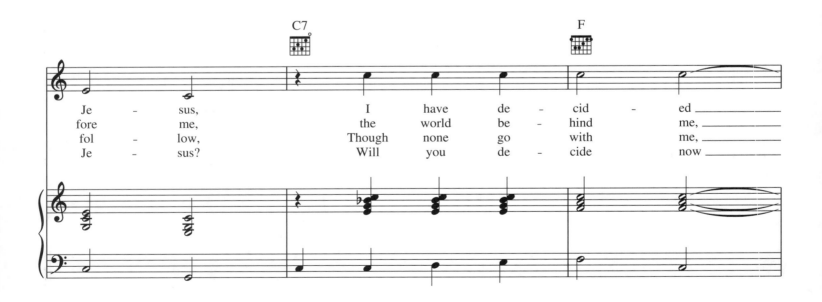

I LOVE THY KINGDOM, LORD

Words by TIMOTHY DWIGHT
Music from *The Universal Psalmodist*
Adapted by AARON WILLIAMS

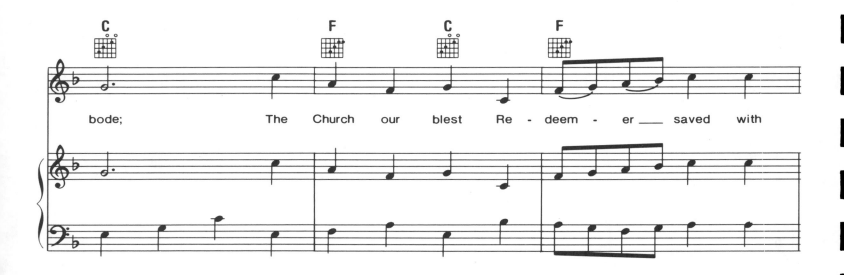

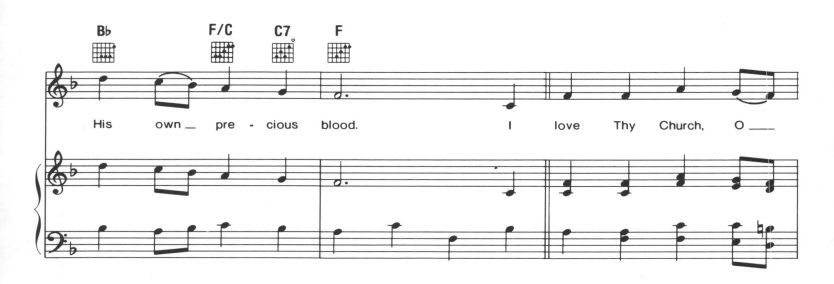

I LOVE TO TELL THE STORY

Words by A. CATHERINE HANKEY
Music by WILLIAM G. FISCHER

I MUST TELL JESUS

Words and Music by
ELISHA A. HOFFMAN

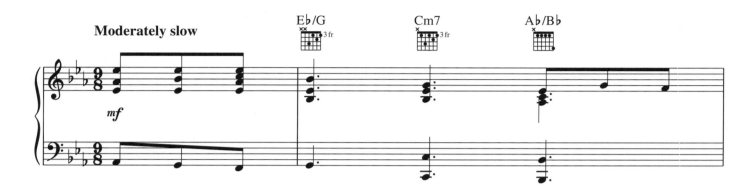

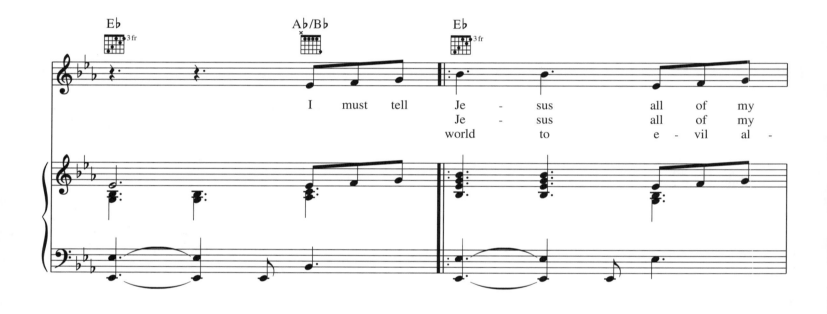

I must tell Je - sus all of my
Je - sus all of my
world to e - vil al -

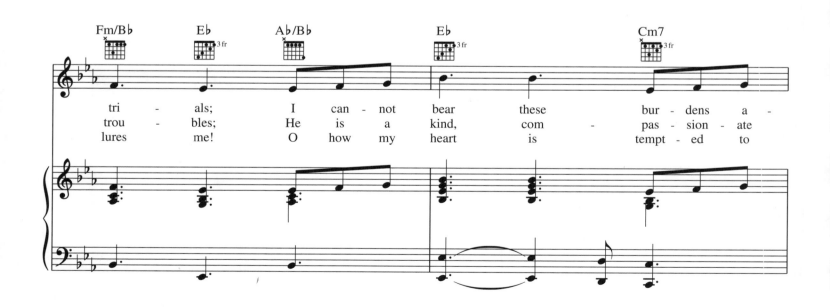

tri - als; I can - not bear these bur - dens a -
trou - bles; He is a kind, com - pas - sion - ate
lures me! O how my heart is tempt - ed to

I SURRENDER ALL

Words by J.W. VAN DEVENTER
Music by W.S. WEEDEN

I NEED THEE EVERY HOUR

Words by ANNIE S. HAWKS
Music by ROBERT LOWRY

I SING THE MIGHTY POWER OF GOD

Words by ISAAC WATTS
Music from *Gesangbuch der Herzogl*

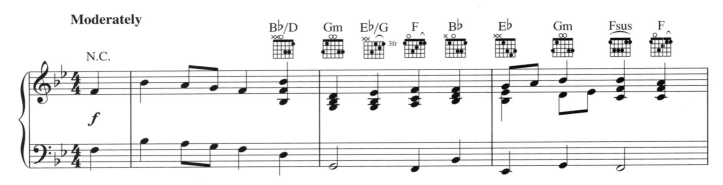

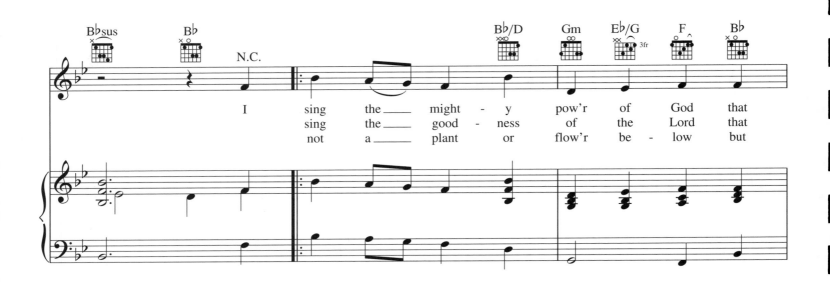

I sing the ___ might - y pow'r of God that
sing the ___ good - ness of the Lord that
not a ___ plant or flow'r be - low but

made ___ the moun - tains rise, that spread the ___ flow - ing
filled ___ the earth with food. He formed the ___ crea - tures
makes ___ Thy glo - ries known. And clouds a - rise and

I STAND AMAZED IN THE PRESENCE
(My Savior's Love)

Words and Music by
CHARLES H. GABRIEL

I WILL SING THE WONDROUS STORY

Words by FRANCIS H. ROWLEY
Music by PETER P. BILHORN

I WOULD BE TRUE

Words by HOWARD A. WALTER
Music by JOSEPH Y. PEEK

I'VE FOUND A FRIEND, O SUCH A FRIEND!

Words by JAMES G. SMALL
Music by GEORGE C. STEBBINS

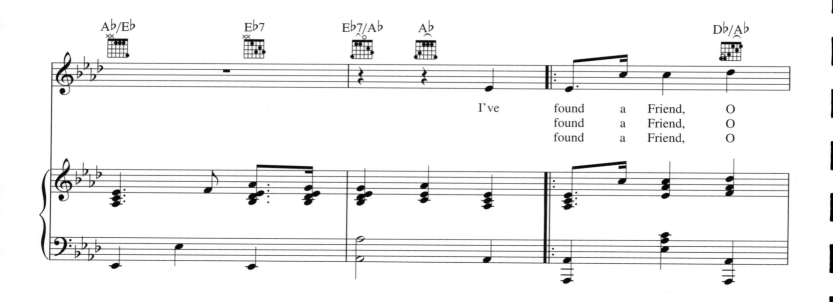

I've found a Friend, O
found a Friend, O
found a Friend, O

such a Friend! He loved me ere I knew Him. He
such a Friend! He bled, He died to save me. And
such a Friend! So kind and true and ten- der, so

I'VE GOT PEACE LIKE A RIVER

Traditional

IMMORTAL, INVISIBLE

Words by WALTER CHALMERS SMITH
Traditional Welsh Melody

IN THE CROSS OF CHRIST I GLORY

Words by JOHN BOWRING
Music by ITHAMAR CONKEY

IN THE GARDEN

Words and Music by
C. AUSTIN MILES

I come to the gar-den a-lone, _____ while the
speaks, and the sound of His voice _____ is so

dew is still on the ros - es; and the voice I
sweet the birds hush their sing - ing; and the mel - o -

hear, fall-ing on my ear, the Son of God dis-
-dy that He gave to me with - in my heart is

IN THE HOUR OF TRIAL

Words by JAMES MONTGOMERY
Altered by FRANCES A. HUTTON
Music by SPENCER LANE

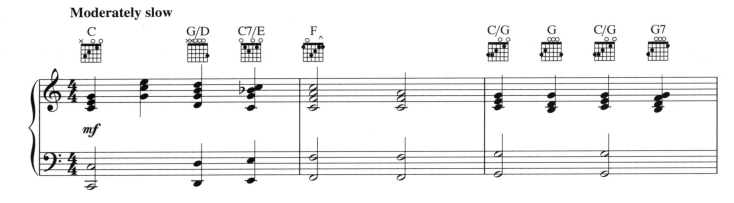

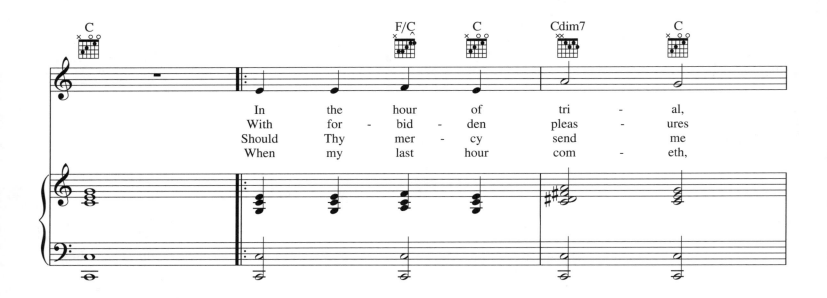

In the hour of tri - al,
With for - bid - den pleas - ures
Should Thy mer - cy send me
When my last hour com - eth,

Je - sus, plead for me, lest by base de -
should this vain world charm, or its base sor - did
sor - row, toil and woe, or should pain at -
fraught with strife and pain, when my dust re -

IT IS WELL WITH MY SOUL

Text by HORATIO G. SPAFFORD
Music by PHILIP P. BLISS

JESUS CALLS US O'ER THE TUMULT

Words by CECIL FRANCES ALEXANDER
Music by WILLIAM H. JUDE

JESUS, THE VERY THOUGHT OF THEE

Words attributed to BERNARD OF CLAIRVAUX
Translated by EDWARD CASWALL
Music by JOHN BACCHUS DYKES

JESUS IS ALL THE WORLD TO ME

Words and Music by
WILL L. THOMPSON

Je - sus is all the world to me, My
Je - sus is all the world to me, My
Je - sus is all the world to me, And
Je - sus is all the world to me, I

life, my joy, my all. ____ He is my strength from day to day; With -
friend in tri - als sore. ____ I go to Him for bless - ings, and He
true to Him I'll be. ____ Oh, how could I this friend de - ny, When
want no bet - ter friend. ____ I trust Him now, I'll trust Him when Life's

JESUS IS TENDERLY CALLING

Words by FANNY J. CROSBY
Music by GEORGE C. STEBBINS

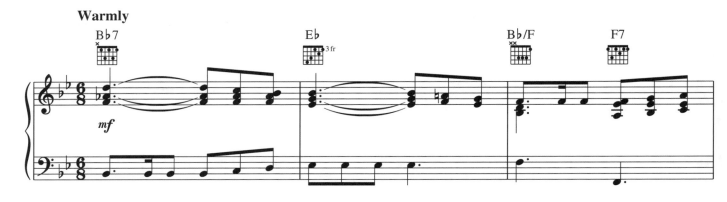

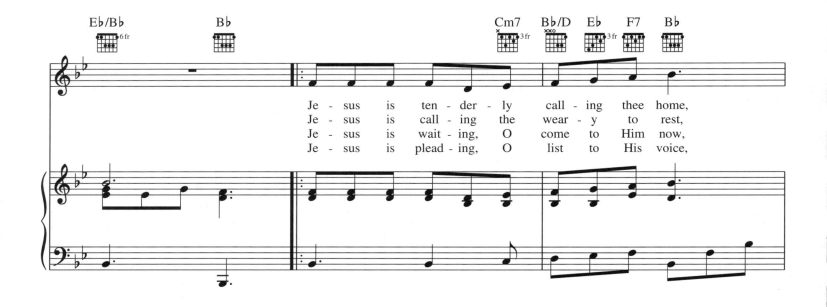

Je - sus is ten - der - ly call - ing thee home,
Je - sus is call - ing the wear - y to rest,
Je - sus is wait - ing, O come to Him now,
Je - sus is plead - ing, O list to His voice,

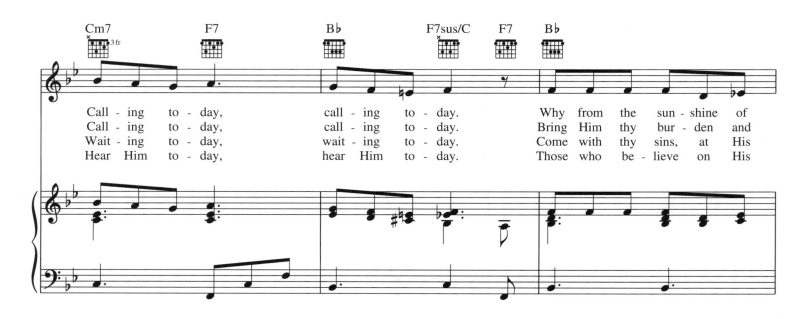

Call - ing to - day, call - ing to - day. Why from the sun - shine of
Call - ing to - day, call - ing to - day. Bring Him thy bur - den and
Wait - ing to - day, wait - ing to - day. Come with thy sins, at His
Hear Him to - day, hear Him to - day. Those who be - lieve on His

209

JESUS, KEEP ME NEAR THE CROSS

Words by FANNY J. CROSBY
Music by WILLIAM H. DOANE

JESUS, LOVER OF MY SOUL

Words by CHARLES WESLEY
Music by SIMEON B. MARSH

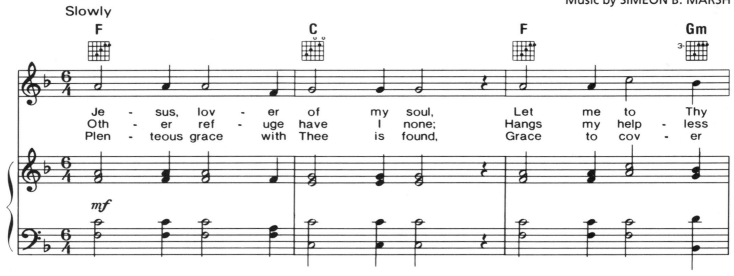

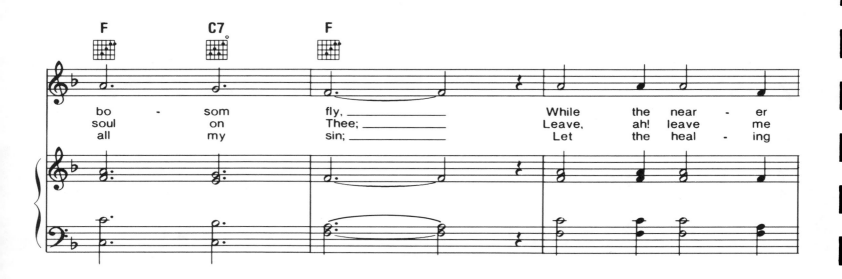

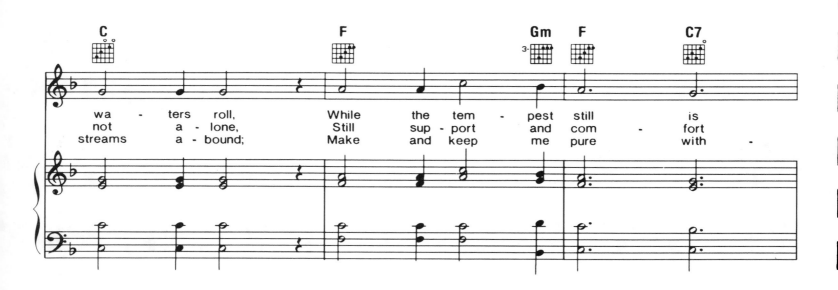

JESUS PAID IT ALL

Words by ELVINA M. HALL
Music by JOHN T. GRAPE

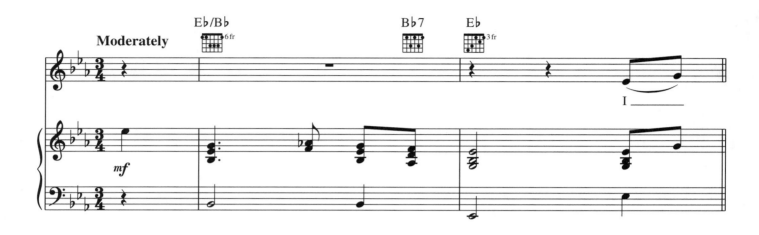

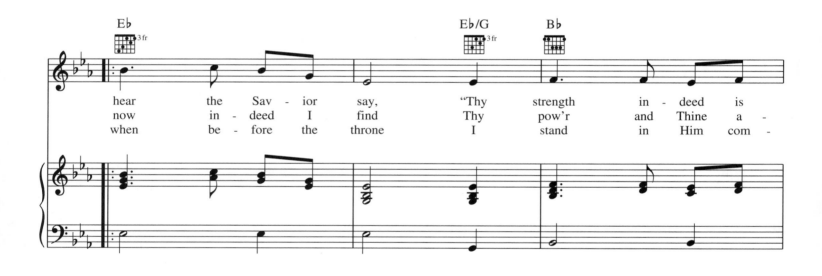

JESUS SAVES!

Words by PRISCILLA J. OWENS
Music by WILLIAM J. KIRKPATRICK

We have heard the joy - ful sound— Je - sus saves! Je - sus
on the roll - ing tide— Je - sus saves! Je - sus
bove the bat - tle strife— Je - sus saves! Je - sus
winds a might - y voice— Je - sus saves! Je - sus

saves! Spread the tid - ings all a - round— Je - sus
saves! Tell to sin - ners far and wide— Je - sus
saves! By His death and end - less life— Je - sus
saves! Let the na - tions now re - joice— Je - sus

JESUS, SAVIOR, PILOT ME

Words by EDWARD HOPPER
Music by JOHN E. GOULD

JESUS SHALL REIGN

Words by ISAAC WATTS
Music by JOHN HATTON

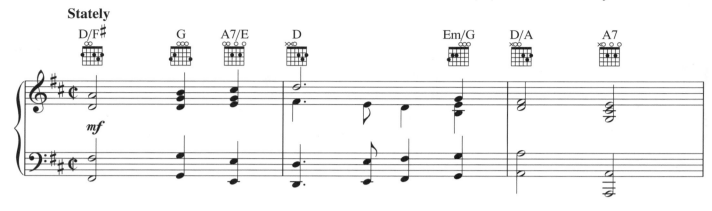

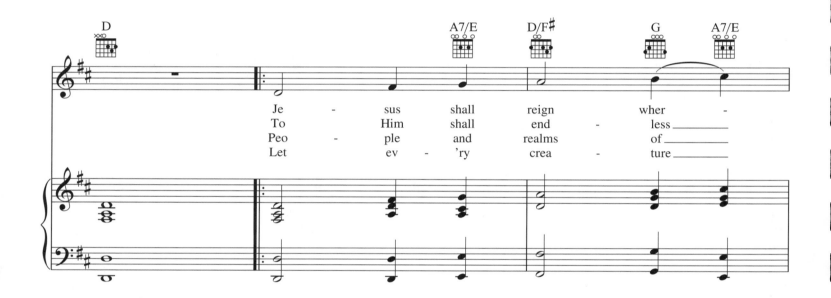

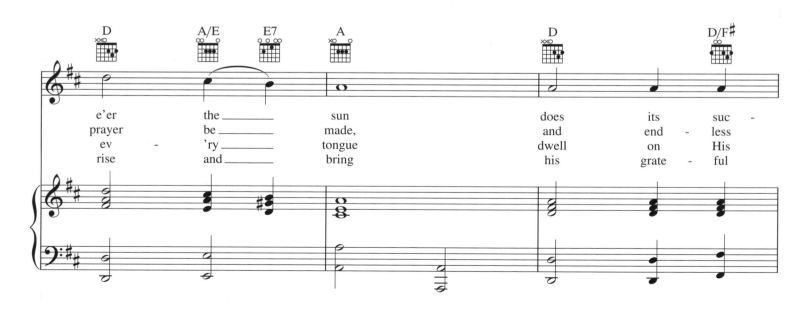

JESUS, THOU JOY OF LOVING HEARTS

Words attributed to BERNARD OF CLAIRVAUX
Translated by RAY PALMER
Music by HENRY BAKER

JESUS WALKED THIS LONESOME VALLEY

Traditional Spiritual

JUST AS I AM

Words by CHARLOTTE ELLIOTT
Music by WILLIAM B. BRADBURY

Slowly, with movement

Just _ as I am, __ with - out __ one plea, But that __ Thy blood was
as I am, __ and wait - ing not To rid __ my soul was of
as I am, __ though tossed a - bout With many _ a con - flict,

shed for me, And _ that Thou bidd'st __ me come to Thee, __ O
one dark blot, To _ Thee whose blood __ can cleanse each spot, __ O
many a doubt, Fight - ings and fears __ with - in, with - out __ O

Lamb of God! __ I come, I come! _____ Just _
Lamb of God! __ I come, I come! _____ Just _
Lamb of God! __ I come, I come! _____

JOYFUL, JOYFUL, WE ADORE THEE

Words by HENRY VAN DYKE
Music by LUDWIG VAN BEETHOVEN,
melody from *Ninth Symphony*
Adapted by EDWARD HODGES

JUST A CLOSER WALK WITH THEE

Traditional
Arranged by KENNETH MORRIS

3. When my feeble life is o'er,
   Time for me will be no more;
   On that bright eternal shore
   I will walk, dear Lord, close to Thee.

JUST OVER IN THE GLORYLAND

Words by JAMES W. ACUFF
Music by EMMETT S. DEAN

1. I've a home pre-pared where the
2.-4. *(See additional verses)*

saints a-bide. Just o-ver in the glo-ry-land; And I long to be by my

Sav-ior's side, Just o-ver in the glo-ry-land. Just o - ver in the

Additional Verses

2. I am on my way to those mansions fair,
   Just over in the gloryland;
   There to sing God's praise and His glory share,
   Just over in the gloryland.
   Refrain

3. What a joyful tho't that my Lord I'll see,
   Just over in the gloryland;
   And with kindred saved there forever be,
   Just over in the gloryland.
   Refrain

4. With the blood-washed throng I will shout and sing,
   Just over in the gloryland;
   Glad hosannas to Christ, the Lord and King,
   Just over in the gloryland.
   Refrain

THE KING OF LOVE MY SHEPHERD IS

Words by HENRY BAKER
Traditional Irish Melody

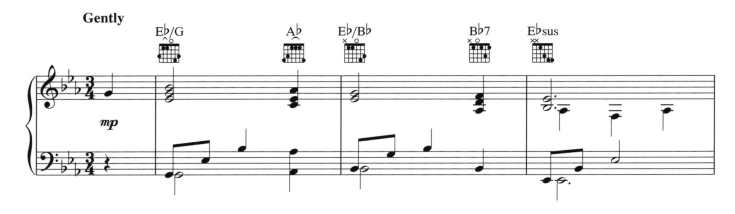

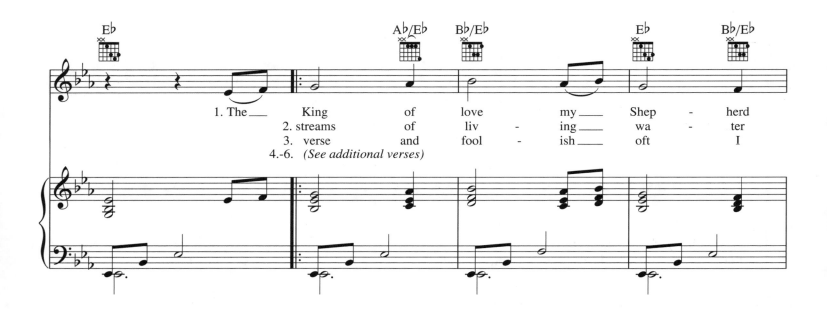

1. The ___ King of love my ___ Shep - herd
2. streams of liv - ing ___ wa - ter
3. verse and fool - ish ___ oft I
4.-6. *(See additional verses)*

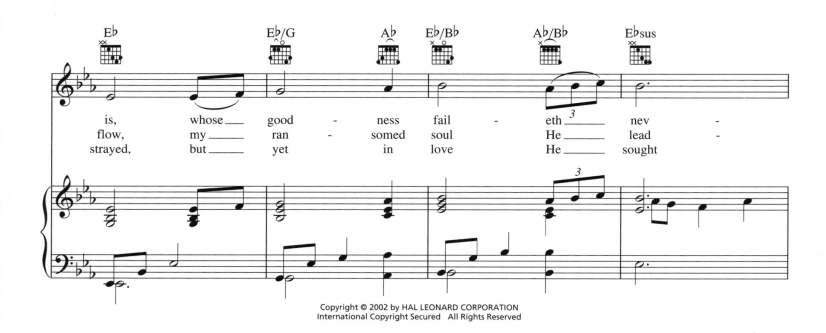

is, whose ___ good - ness fail - eth nev -
flow, my ___ ran - somed soul He ___ lead -
strayed, but ___ yet in love He ___ sought

Additional Verses

4. In death's dark vale I fear no ill
   With Thee, dear Lord, beside me.
   Thy rod and staff my comfort still,
   Thy cross before to guide me.

5. Thou spreadst a table in my sight,
   Thine unction grace bestoweth.
   And O what transport of delight
   From Thy pure chalice floweth!

6. And so through all the length of days
   Thy goodness faileth never.
   Good Shepherd, may I sing Thy praise
   Within Thy house forever.

KUM BA YAH

Traditional Spiritual

LEANING ON
THE EVERLASTING ARMS

Words by ELISHA A. HOFFMAN
Music by ANTHONY J. SHOWALTER

LEAD ON, O KING ETERNAL

Words by ERNEST W. SHURTLEFF
Music by HENRY T. SMART

Lead on, O King e - ter - nal, The
on, O King e - ter - nal, Till
on, O King e - ter - nal, We

day of march has come; Hence - forth in fields of
sin's fierce war shall cease, And ho - li - ness shall
fol - low, not with fears; For glad - ness breaks like

LET ALL MORTAL FLESH KEEP SILENCE

Words from *The Liturgy of St. James*
Translated by GERARD MOULTRIE
17th Century French Carol

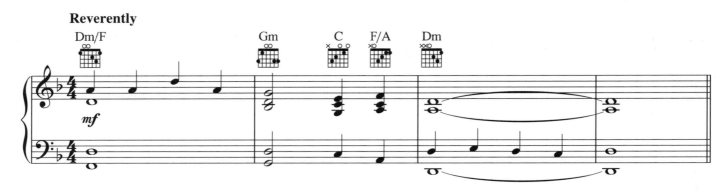

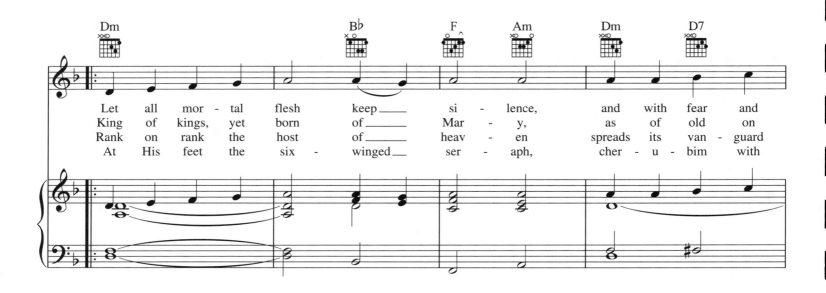

Let all mor - tal flesh keep si - lence, and with fear and
King of kings, yet born of Mar - y, as of old on
Rank on rank the host of heav - en spreads its van - guard
At His feet the six - winged ser - aph, cher - u - bim with

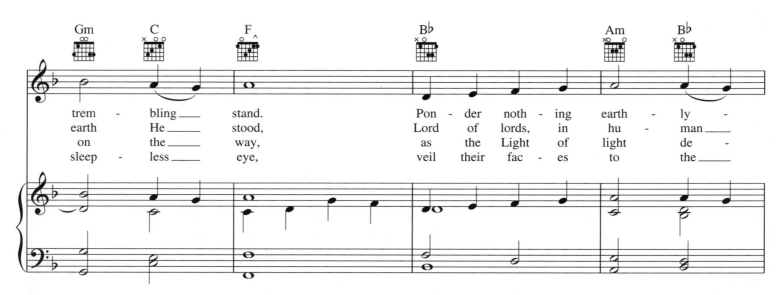

trem - bling stand. Pon - der noth - ing earth - ly -
earth He stood, Lord of lords, in hu - man -
on the way, as the Light of light de -
sleep - less eye, veil their fac - es to the

LET US BREAK BREAD TOGETHER

Traditional Spiritual

LIFT EV'RY VOICE AND SING

Words by JAMES WELDON JOHNSON
Music by J. ROSAMOND JOHNSON

LIFE'S RAILWAY TO HEAVEN

Words by M.E. ABBEY
Music by CHARLES D. TILLMAN

THE LILY OF THE VALLEY

Words by CHARLES W. FRY
Music by WILLIAM S. HAYS

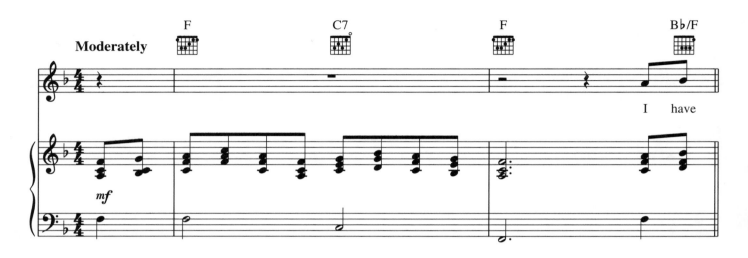

I have

found a friend in Je - sus, He's ev - 'ry - thing to me, He's the
all my grief has tak - en, and all my sor - rows borne; In temp -
nev - er, nev - er leave me, nor yet for - sake me here, While I

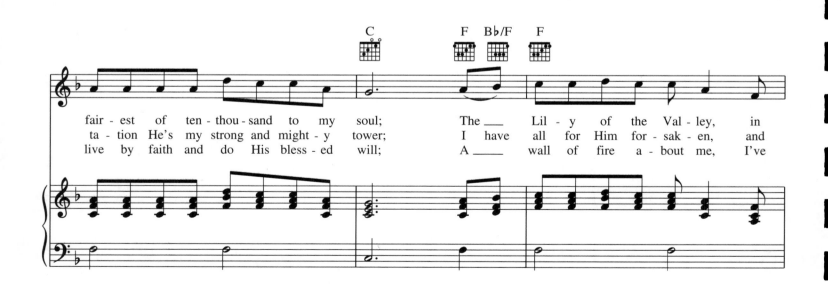

fair - est of ten - thou - sand to my soul; The ___ Lil - y of the Val - ley, in
ta - tion He's my strong and might - y tow - er; I have all for Him for - sak - en, and
live by faith and do His bless - ed will; A ___ wall of fire a - bout me, I've

THE LORD BLESS YOU AND KEEP YOU

Words and Music by
PETER C. LUTKIN

LORD, I WANT TO BE A CHRISTIAN

Traditional Spiritual

NOBODY KNOWS
THE TROUBLE I'VE SEEN

African-American Spiritual

THE LORD'S MY SHEPHERD, I'LL NOT WANT

Words from *Scottish Psalter*, 1650
Based on Psalm 23
Music by JESSIE S. IRVINE

LOVE DIVINE, ALL LOVES EXCELLING

Words by CHARLES WESLEY
Music by JOHN ZUNDEL

LOVE LIFTED ME

Words by JAMES ROWE
Music by HOWARD E. SMITH

A MIGHTY FORTRESS IS OUR GOD

Words and Music by MARTIN LUTHER
Translated by FREDERICK H. HEDGE
Based on Psalm 46

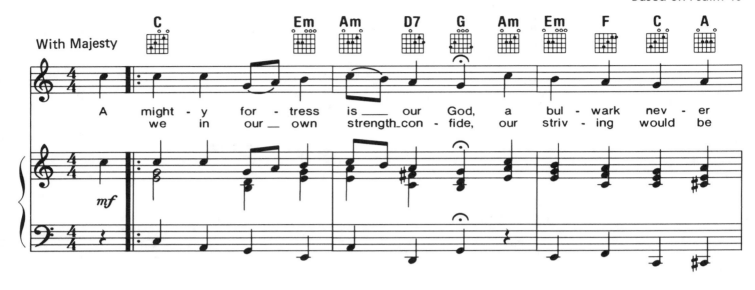

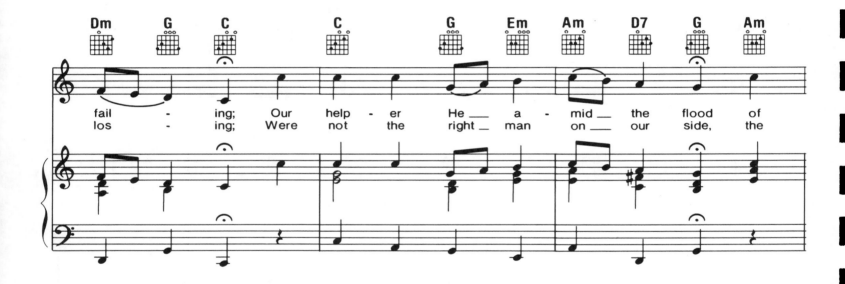

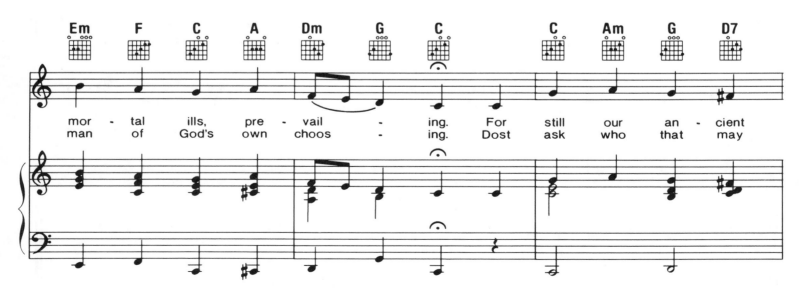

Additional Verses

3. And tho this world, with devils filled,
Should threaten to undo us;
We will not fear, for God hath willed
His truth to triumph through us;
The Prince of darkness grim,
We tremble not for him;
His rage we can endure,
For lo! His doom is sure,
One little word shall fell him.

4. That word above all earthly powers,
No thanks to them abideth,
The spirit and the gifts are ours
Through Him who with us sideth;
Let goods and kindred go,
This mortal life also;
The body they may kill;
God's truth abideth still,
His kingdom is forever.

MORE LOVE TO THEE

Words by ELIZABETH PAYSON PRENTISS
Music by WILLIAM H. DOANE

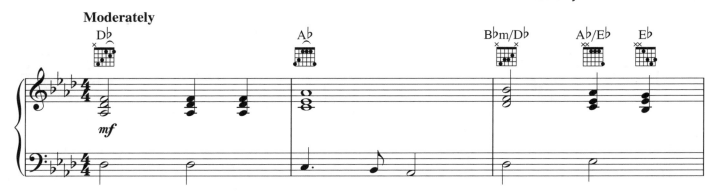

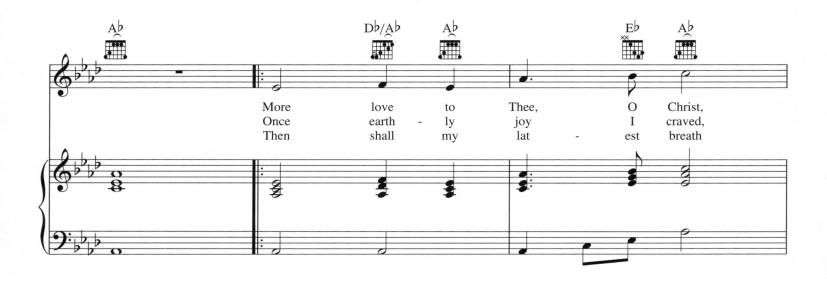

More love to Thee, O Christ,
Once earth-ly joy I craved,
Then shall my lat-est breath

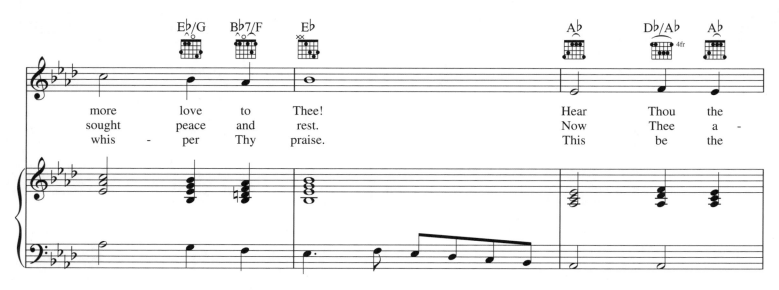

more love to Thee!
sought peace and rest.
whis-per and Thy praise.

Hear Thou the
Now Thee a-
This be the

MUST JESUS BEAR THE CROSS ALONE

Words by THOMAS SHEPHERD
Music by GEORGE N. ALLEN

Moderately

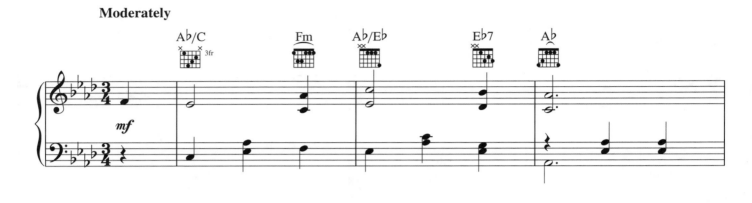

Must Je - sus bear the cross a -
con - se - crat - ed cross I'll
on the crys - tal pave - ment,
pre - cious cross! O glo - rious

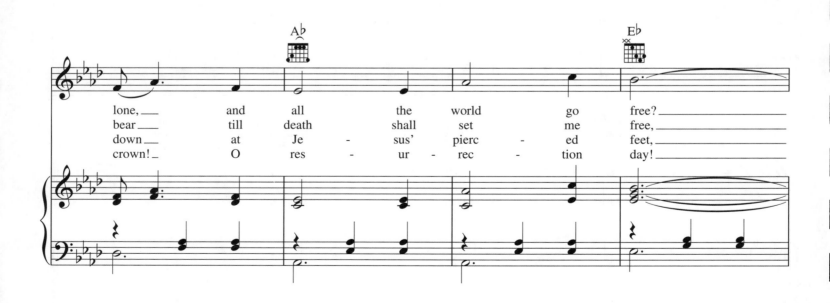

lone, and all the world go free?
bear till death shall set me free,
down at Je - sus' pierc - ed feet,
crown! O res - ur - rec - tion day!

MY FAITH HAS FOUND A RESTING PLACE

Words by LIDIE H. EDMUNDS
Music by ANDRÉ GRÉTRY
Arranged by WILLIAM J. KIRKPATRICK

MY FAITH LOOKS UP TO THEE

Words by RAY PALMER
Music by LOWELL MASON

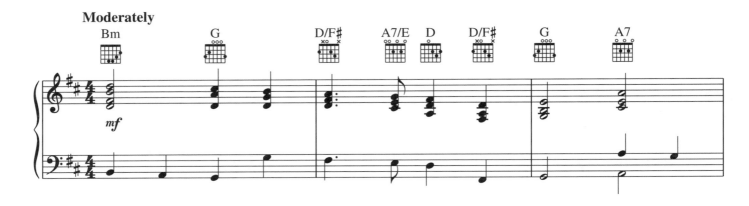

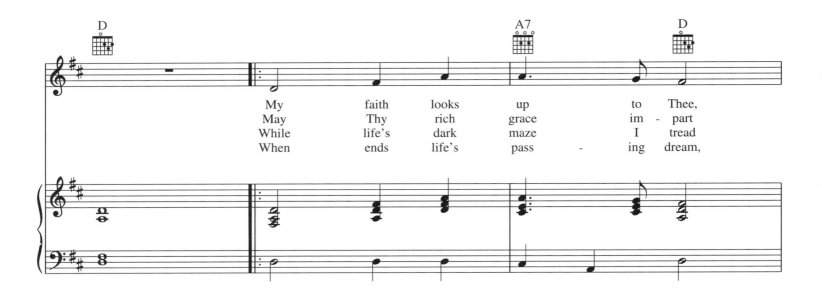

My faith looks up to Thee,
May Thy rich grace im - part
While life's dark maze I tread
When ends life's pass - ing dream,

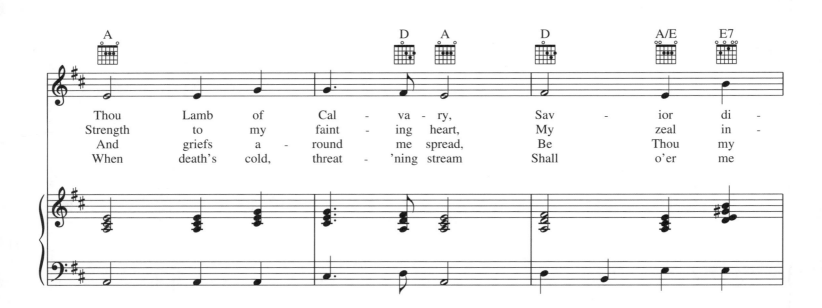

Thou Lamb of Cal - va - ry, Sav - ior di -
Strength to my faint - ing heart, My zeal in -
And griefs a - round me spread, Be Thou my
When death's cold, threat - 'ning stream Shall o'er me

MY HOPE IS BUILT ON NOTHING LESS

Words by EDWARD MOTE
Music by WILLIAM B. BRADBURY

MY JESUS, I LOVE THEE

Words by WILLIAM R. FEATHERSTON
Music by ADONIRAM J. GORDON

My Je - sus, I love _____ Thee, I
love Thee be - cause _____ Thou hast
love Thee in life, _____ I will
man - sions of glo - ry and

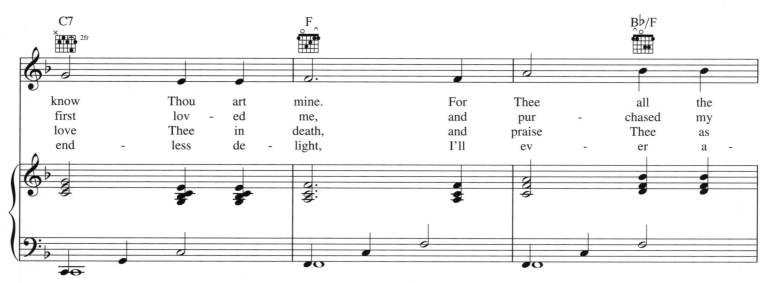

know Thou art mine. For Thee all the
first lov - ed me, and Thee pur - chased my
love Thee in death, and praise Thee as
end - less de - light, I'll ev - er a -

MY SAVIOR FIRST OF ALL

Words by FANNY J. CROSBY
Music by JOHN R. SWENEY

NEAR TO THE HEART OF GOD

Words and Music by
CLELAND B. McAFEE

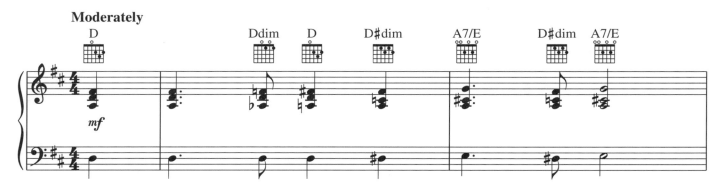

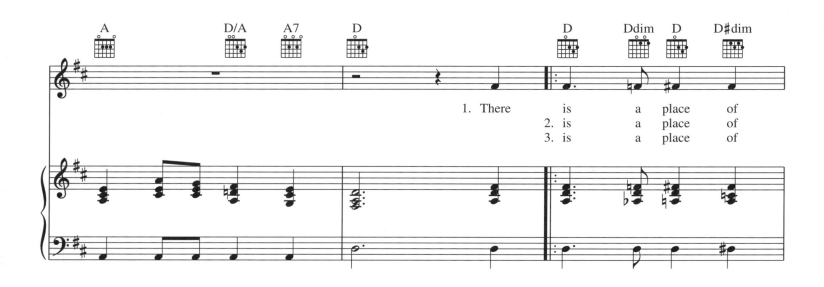

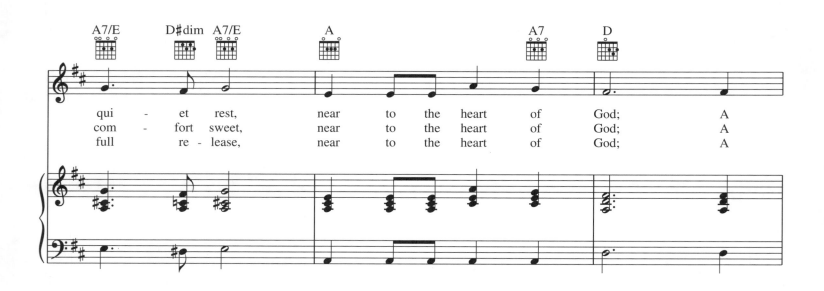

1. There is a place of qui - et rest, near to the heart of God; A
2. is a place of com - fort sweet, near to the heart of God; A
3. is a place of full re - lease, near to the heart of God; A

NEARER, MY GOD, TO THEE

Words by SARAH F. ADAMS
Based on Genesis 28:10-22
Music by LOWELL MASON

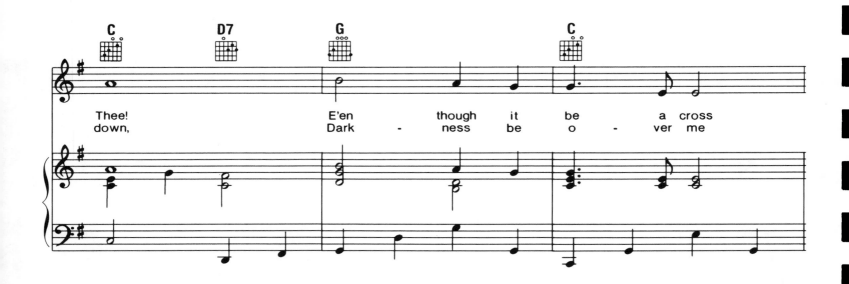

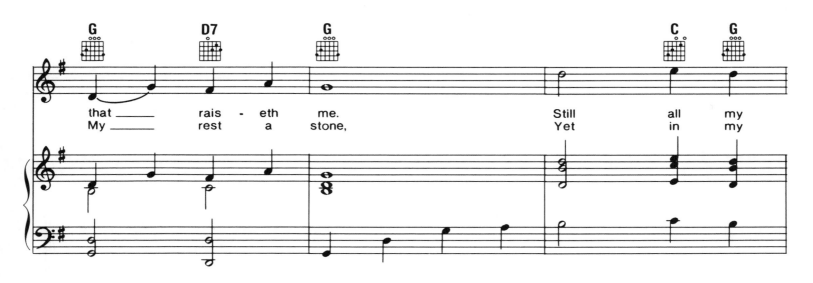

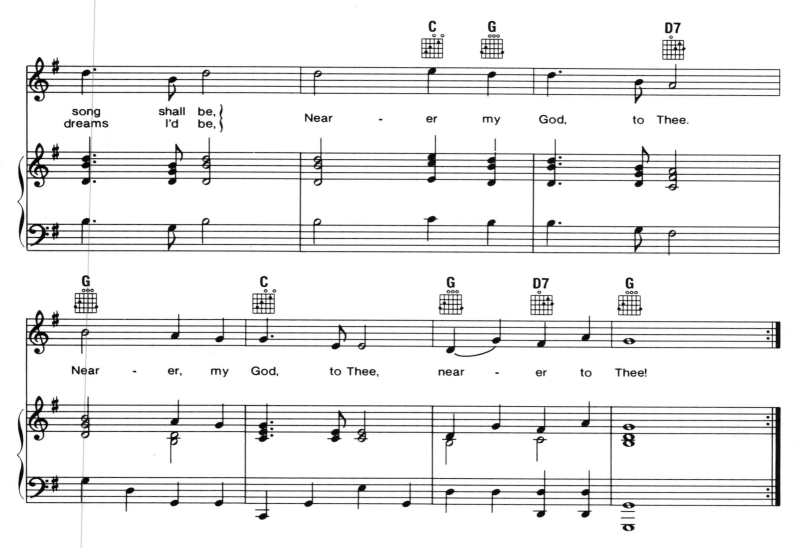

C G   D7

song   shall be,⎫
dreams I'd   be,⎭   Near - er my God, to Thee.

G   C   G   D7   G

Near - er, my God, to Thee, near - er to Thee!

3. Then with my waking tho'ts
Bright with Thy praise,
Out of my stony griefs
Bethel I'll raise
So by my woes to be,
Nearer, my God, to Thee,
Nearer, my God, to Thee,
Nearer to Thee!

4. Or if on joyful wing,
Cleaving the sky,
Sun, moon, and stars forgot,
Upwards I'll fly,
Still all my song shall be,
Nearer, my God, to Thee,
Nearer, my God, to Thee,
Nearer to Thee!

NEVER SAID A MUMBLIN' WORD

African-American Spiritual

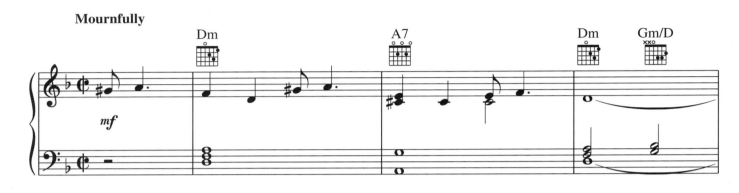

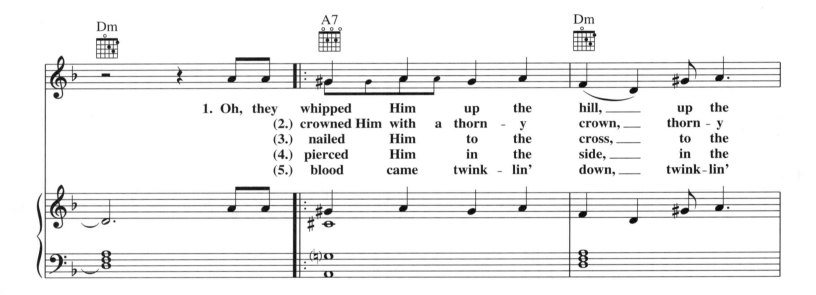

1. Oh, they whipped Him up the hill, _____ up the
(2.) crowned Him with a thorn - y crown, _____ thorn - y
(3.) nailed Him to the cross, _____ to the
(4.) pierced Him in the side, _____ in the
(5.) blood came twink - lin' down, _____ twink-lin'

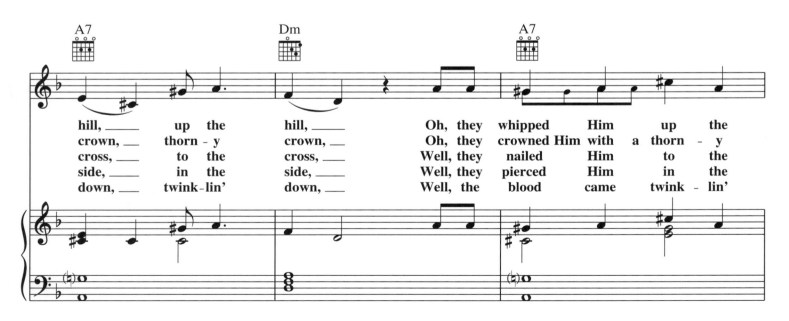

hill, _____ up the hill, _____ Oh, they whipped Him up the
crown, _____ thorn - y crown, _____ Oh, they crowned Him with a thorn - y
cross, _____ to the cross, _____ Well, they nailed Him to the
side, _____ in the side, _____ Well, they pierced Him in the
down, _____ twink - lin' down, _____ Well, the blood came twink - lin'

NOTHING BUT THE BLOOD

Words and Music by
ROBERT LOWRY

Additional Verses

2. For my pardon this I see
   Nothing but the blood of Jesus;
   For my cleansing this my plea
   Nothing but the blood of Jesus.
   Refrain

3. Nothing can for sin atone
   Nothing but the blood of Jesus;
   Naught of good that I have done
   Nothing but the blood of Jesus.
   Refrain

NOW THANK WE ALL OUR GOD

German Words by MARTIN RINKART
English Translation by CATHERINE WINKWORTH
Music by JOHANN CRÜGER

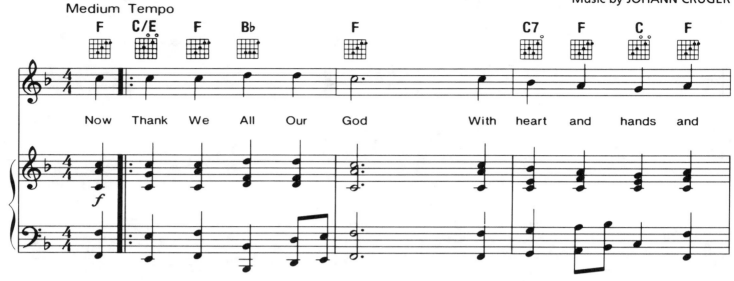

Now Thank We All Our God   With heart and hands and

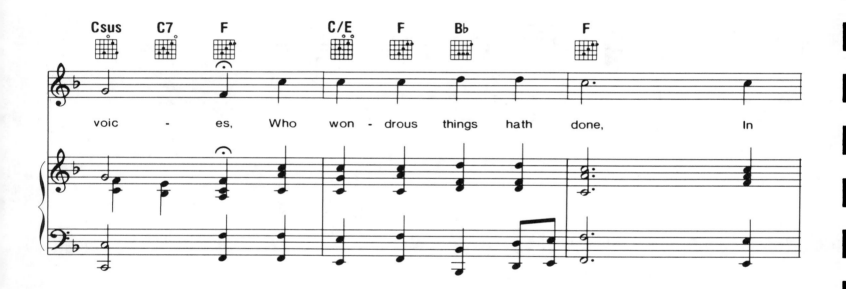

voic - es, Who won - drous things hath done,   In

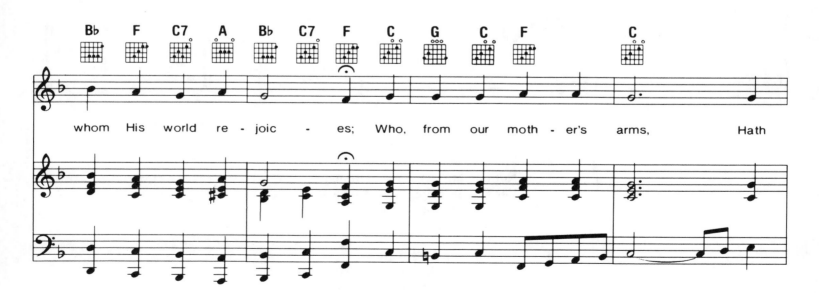

whom His world re - joic - es; Who, from our moth - er's arms,   Hath

blessed us on our way With count - less gifts of

love, And still is ours to - day. O more.

Additional Verses

2. (O) may this bounteous God
Through all our life be near us,
With ever joyful hearts
And blessed peace to cheer us;
And keep us in His grace,
And guide us when perplexed,
And free us from all ills,
In this world and the next.

3. (All) praise and thanks to God
The Father now be given,
The Son and Him who reigns
With them in highest heaven;
The one eternal God,
Whom earth and heav'n adore;
For thus it was, is now,
And shall be evermore.

NOW THE DAY IS OVER

Words by SABINE BARING-GOULD
Music by JOSEPH BARNBY

O FOR A THOUSAND TONGUES TO SING

Words by CHARLES WESLEY
Music by CARL G. GLÄSER

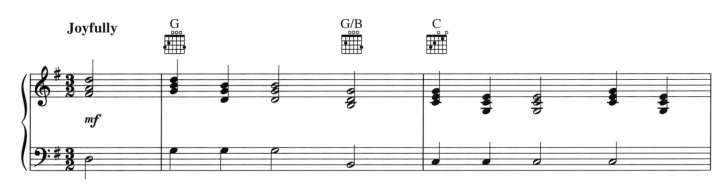

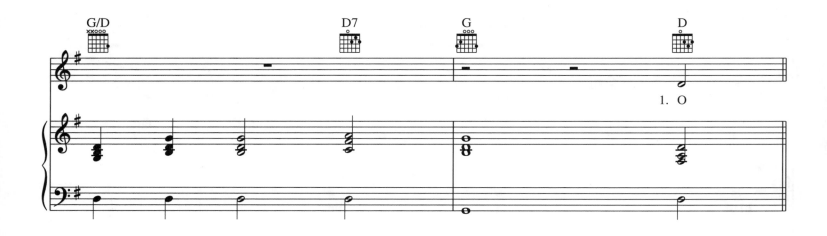

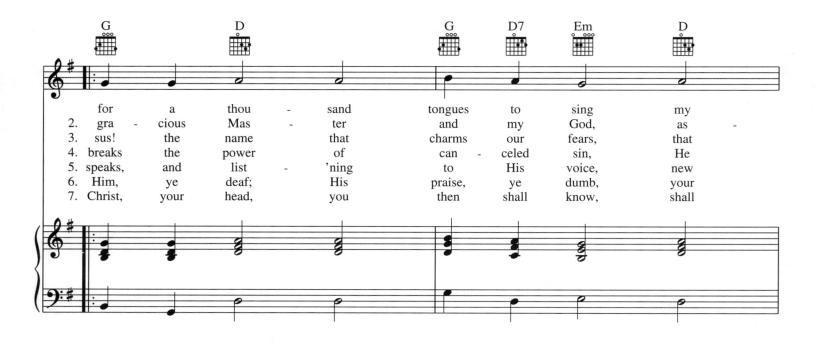

1. O for a thou - sand tongues to sing my
2. gra - cious Mas - ter and my God, as -
3. sus! the name that charms our fears, that
4. breaks the power of can - celed sin, He
5. speaks, and list - 'ning to His voice, new
6. Him, ye deaf; His praise, ye dumb, your
7. Christ, your head, you then shall know, your

O GOD, OUR HELP IN AGES PAST

Words by ISAAC WATTS
Music by WILLIAM CROFT

O HOW I LOVE JESUS

Words by FREDERICK WHITFIELD
Traditional American Melody

There is a name __ I love to hear, I
tells me of _____ a Sav - ior's love, who
tells me what __ my Fa - ther hath in
tells of One __ whose lov - ing heart can

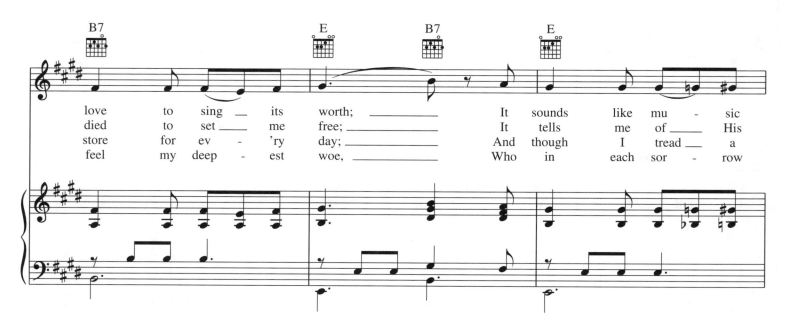

love to sing __ its worth; _____ It sounds like mu - sic
died to set _____ me free; _____ It sounds tells me of _____ His
store for ev - 'ry day; _____ And though I tread __ a
feel my deep - est woe, _____ Who in each sor - row

O JESUS, I HAVE PROMISED

Words by JOHN E. BODE
Music by ARTHUR H. MANN

Lyrics:

O Je - sus, I have prom - ised to serve Thee to the end;
Je - sus, Thou hast prom - ised To all who fol - low Thee,
let me feel Thee near me! The world is ev - er near;
let me hear Thee speak - ing In ac - cents clear and near;

Be Thou for - ev - er near me, My
That where Thou art in glo - ry, There
I see the sights that daz - zle, The
A - bove the storms of pas - sion, The

O LOVE THAT WILT NOT LET ME GO

Words by GEORGE MATHESON
Music by ALBERT LISTER PEACE

ONLY BELIEVE

Words and Music by
PAUL RADER

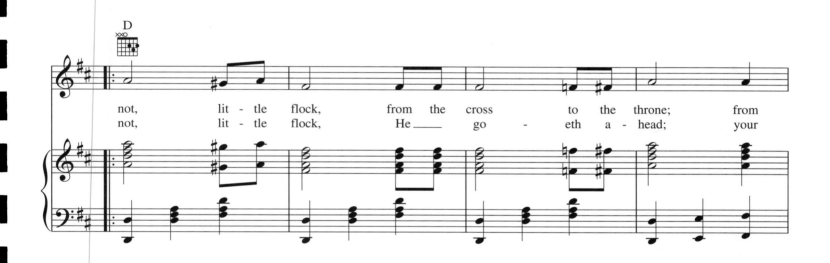

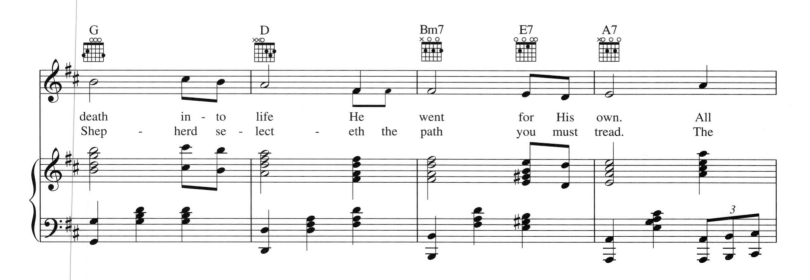

O MASTER, LET ME WALK WITH THEE

Words by WASHINGTON GLADDEN
Music by H. PERCY SMITH

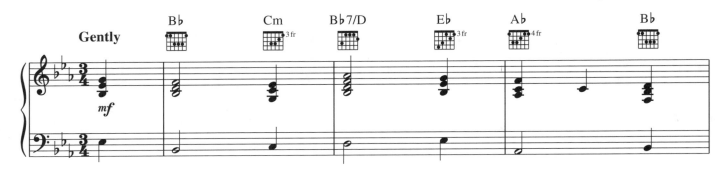

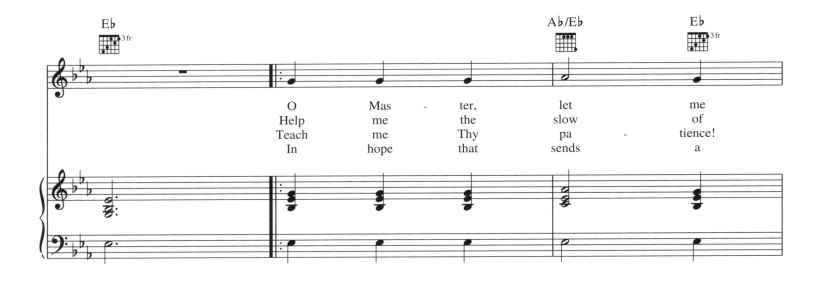

O Master, let me
Help me the slow of
Teach me Thy patience!
In hope that sends a

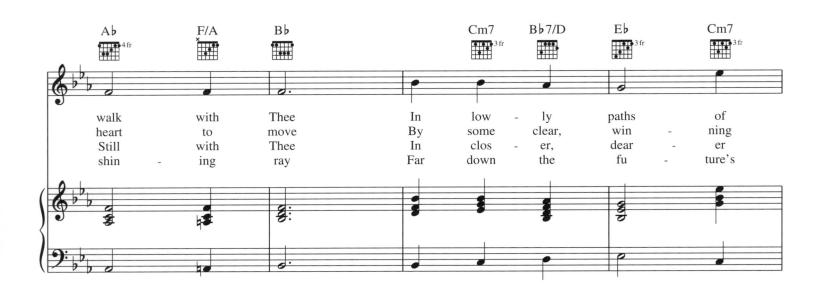

walk with Thee In lowly paths of
heart to move By some clear, win ning
Still with Thee move In clos er, dear er
shin ing ray Far down the fu ture's

O PERFECT LOVE

Words by DOROTHY FRANCES GURNEY
Music by JOSEPH BARNBY

O SACRED HEAD, NOW WOUNDED

Words by BERNARD OF CLAIRVAUX
Music by HANS LEO HASSLER

O WORSHIP THE KING

Words by ROBERT GRANT
Music attributed to JOHANN MICHAEL HAYDN
Arranged by WILLIAM GARDINER

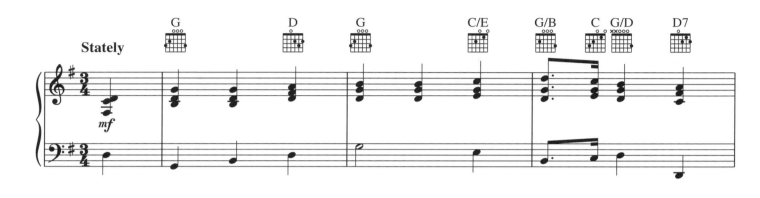

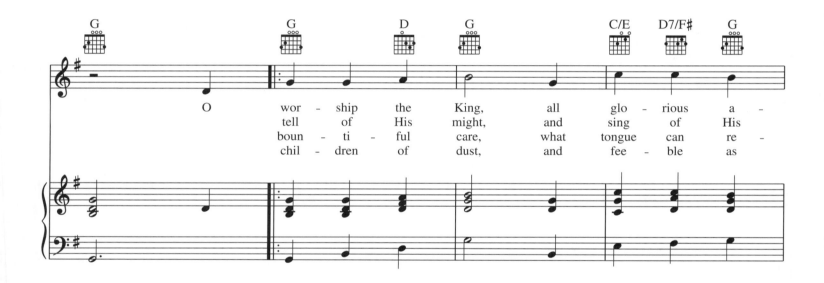

O wor-ship the King, all glo-rious a-
tell of His might, all and sing of His
boun-ti-ful care, what tongue can re-
chil-dren of dust, and fee-ble as

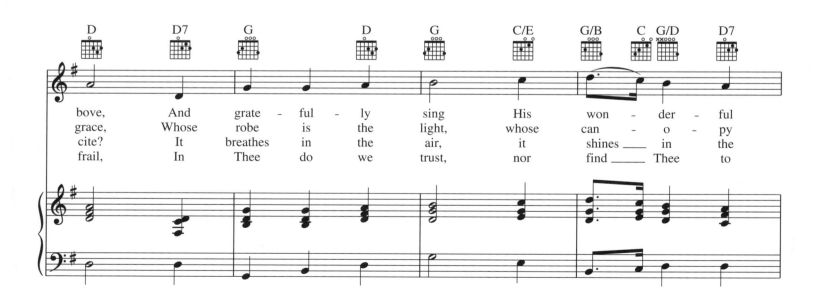

bove, And grate-ful-ly sing His won-der-ful
grace, Whose robe is the light, whose can-o-py
cite? It breathes in the air, it shines ___ in the
frail, In Thee do we trust, nor find ___ Thee to

THE OLD RUGGED CROSS

Words and Music by
REV. GEORGE BENNARD

ON JORDAN'S STORMY BANKS

Words by SAMUEL STENNETT
Traditional American Melody

ONCE TO EVERY MAN AND NATION

Words by JAMES RUSSELL LOWELL
Music by THOMAS J. WILLIAMS

ONLY TRUST HIM

Words and Music by
JOHN H. STOCKTON

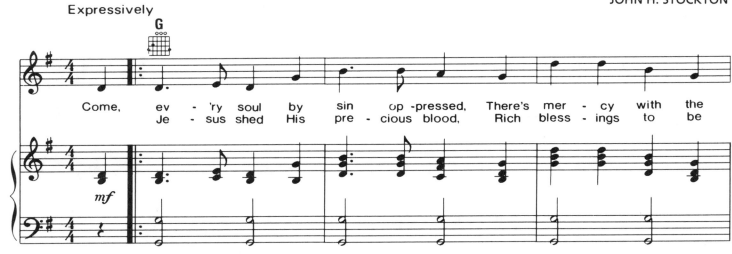

Come, ev - 'ry soul by sin op - pressed, There's mer - cy with the
Je - sus shed His pre - cious blood, Rich bless - ings to be

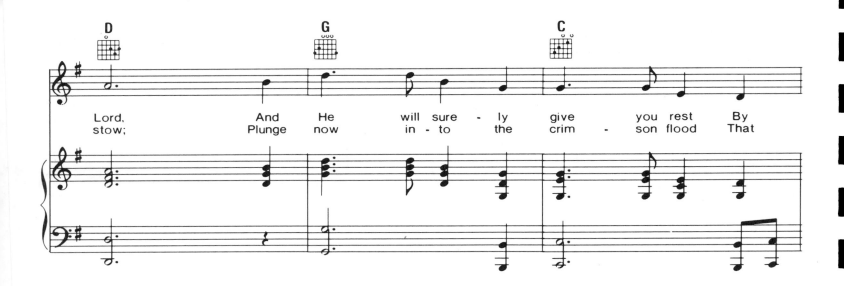

Lord, And He will sure - ly give you rest By
stow; Plunge now in - to the crim - son flood That

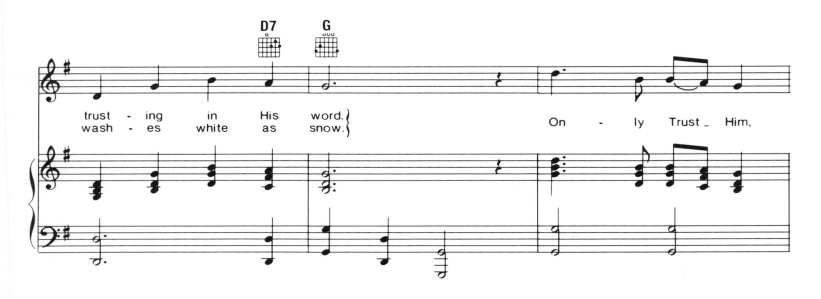

trust - ing in His word.
wash - es white as snow.

On - ly Trust Him,

3. Yes, Jesus is the truth, the way,
   That leads you into rest;
   Believe in Him without delay,
   And you are fully blest.

4. Come, then, and join this holy band,
   And on to glory go,
   To dwell in that celestial land,
   Where joys immortal flow.

ONWARD, CHRISTIAN SOLDIERS

Words by SABINE BARING-GOULD
Music by ARTHUR S. SULLIVAN

March tempo

On - ward, Chris - tian sol - diers march - ing as to
Like a might - y ar - my moves the church of
On - ward, then, ye peo - ple join our hap - py

war with the cross of Je - sus go - ing on be -
God. Broth - ers we are tread - ing where the saints have
throng. Blend with ours your voic - es in the tri - umph

fore! Christ, the roy - al Mas - ter, leads a - gainst the
trod. We are not di - vid - ed, all one bod - y
song. Glo - ry, laud, and hon - or un - to Christ the

OPEN MY EYES, THAT I MAY SEE

Words and Music by CLARA H. SCOTT

O - pen my eyes, that I may see
O - pen my ears, that I may hear
O - pen my mouth and let me bear

glimps - es of truth Thou hast for me.
voic - es of truth Thou send - est clear;
glad - ly the warm truth ev - 'ry - where.

Place in my hands the won - der - ful key
and while the wave - notes fall on my ear,
O - pen my heart and let me pre - pare

PASS ME NOT, O GENTLE SAVIOR

Words by FANNY J. CROSBY
Music by WILLIAM H. DOANE

Refrain

by. Sav - ior, Sav - ior,

hear my hum - ble cry; While on oth - ers Thou art

call - ing, do not pass me by. by.

Additional Verses

2. **Let me at the throne of mercy find a sweet relief;**
   Kneeling there in deep contrition, help my unbelief.
   Refrain

3. **Trusting only in Thy merit, would I seek Thy face;**
   Heal my wounded, broken spirit, save me by Thy grace.
   Refrain

4. **Be the Spring of all my comfort, more than life to me;**
   Not just here on earth beside me, but eternally.
   Refrain

PRAISE GOD, FROM WHOM ALL BLESSINGS FLOW

Words by THOMAS KEN
Music Attributed to LOUIS BOURGEOIS

PRAISE, MY SOUL,
THE KING OF HEAVEN

Text by HENRY F. LYTE
Music by JOHN GOSS

PRAISE THE LORD!
YE HEAVENS, ADORE HIM

Words from *Foundling Hospital Collection*
V.3 by EDWARD OSLER
Music by FRANZ JOSEPH HAYDN

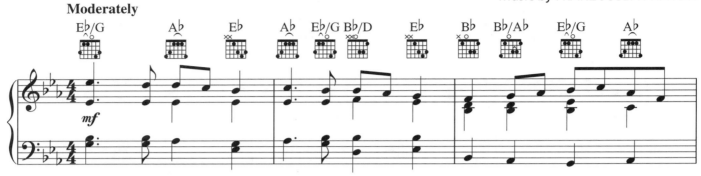

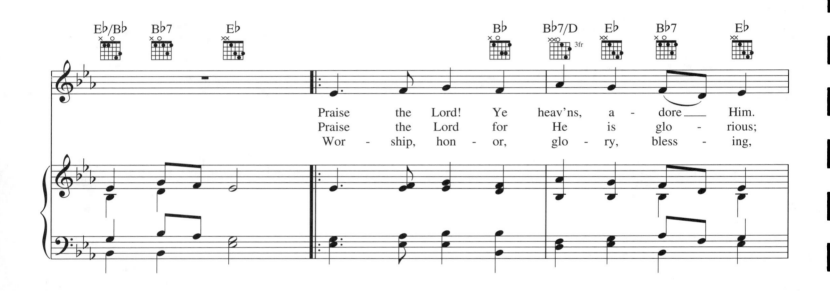

Praise the Lord! Ye heav'ns, a-dore ___ Him.
Praise the Lord For He is glo- rious;
Wor- ship, hon- or, glo- ry, bless- ing,

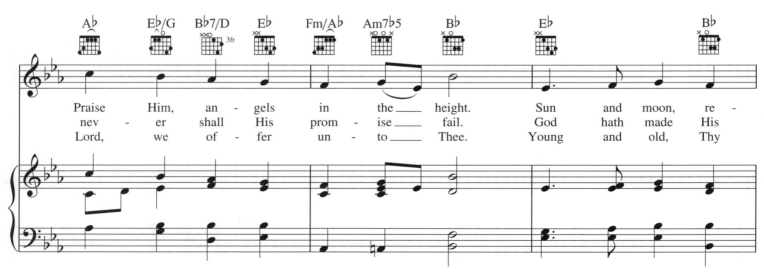

Praise Him, an- gels in the ___ height. Sun and moon, re-
nev- er shall His prom- ise ___ fail. God hath made His
Lord, we of- fer un- to ___ Thee. Young and old, Thy

PRAISE TO THE LORD, THE ALMIGHTY

Words by JOACHIM NEANDER
Translated by CATHERINE WINKWORTH
Music from *Erneuerten Gesangbuch*

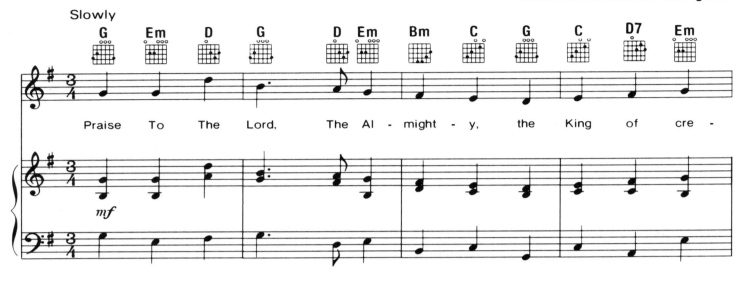

Slowly

Praise To The Lord, The Al - might - y, the King of cre -

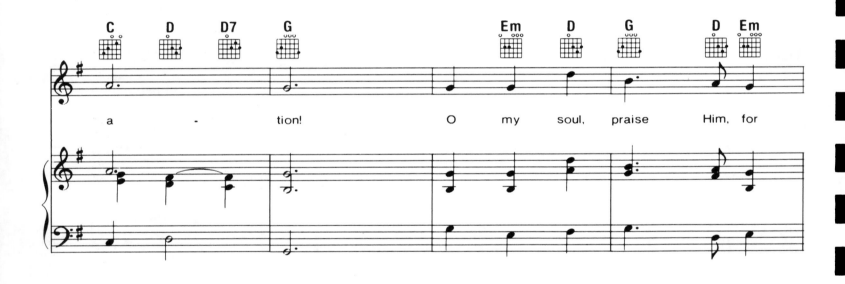

a - tion! O my soul, praise Him, for

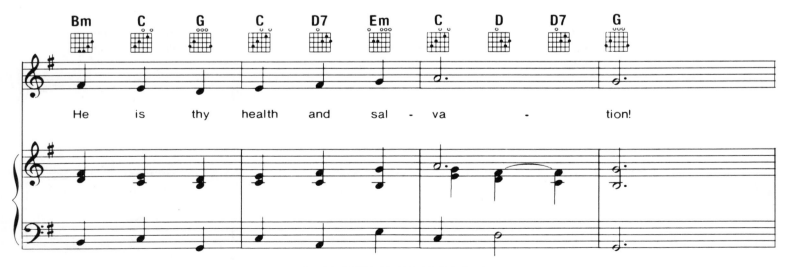

He is thy health and sal - va - tion!

339

PRECIOUS MEMORIES

Words and Music by
J.B.F. WRIGHT

3. As I travel on life's pathway, I know not what life shall hold;
   As I wander hopes grow fonder, Precious mem'ries flood my soul.

REDEEMED

Words by FANNY J. CROSBY
Music by WILLIAM J. KIRKPATRICK

REJOICE, THE LORD IS KING

Words by CHARLES WESLEY
Music by JOHN DARWALL

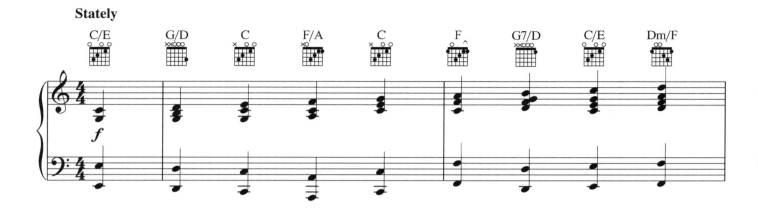

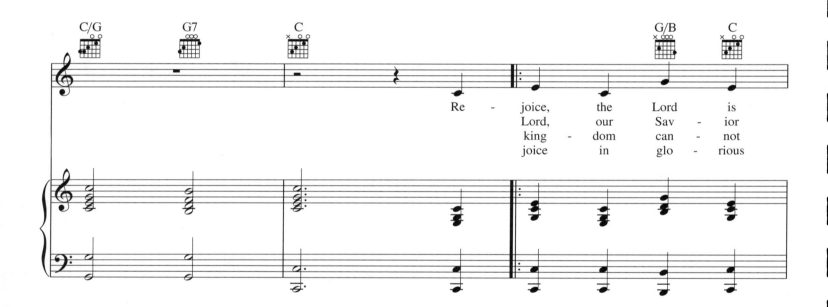

Re - joice, the Lord is
Lord, our Sav - ior
king - dom can - not
joice in glo - rious

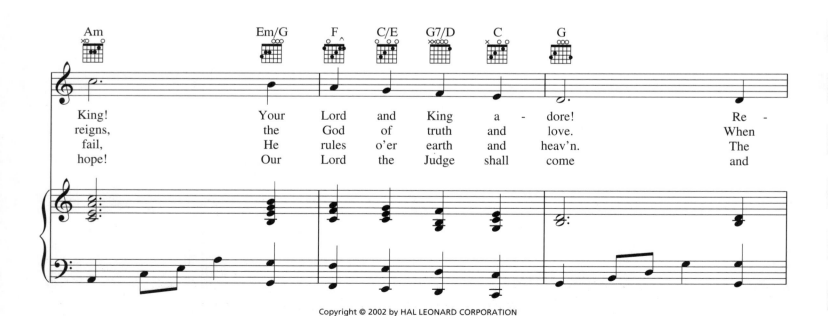

King! Your Lord and King a - dore! Re -
reigns, the God of truth and love. When
fail, He rules o'er earth and heav'n. The
hope! Our Lord the Judge shall come and

REJOICE, YE PURE IN HEART

Words by EDWARD HAYES PLUMPTRE
Music by ARTHUR HENRY MESSITER

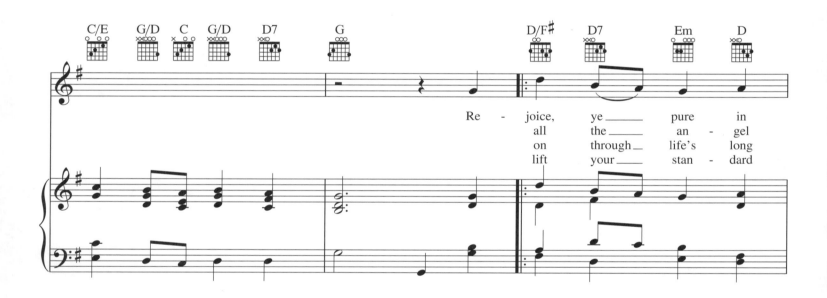

Re - joice, ye _____ pure in
all the _____ an - gel
on through _____ life's long
lift your _____ stan - dard

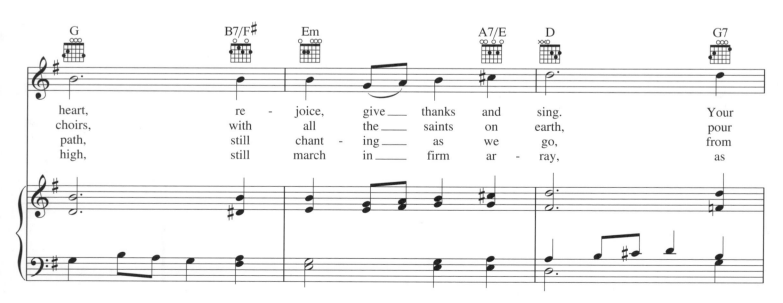

heart, re - joice, give _____ thanks and sing. Your
choirs, with all the _____ saints on earth, pour
path, still chant - ing _____ as we go, from
high, still march in _____ firm ar - ray, as

REVIVE US AGAIN

Words by WILLIAM P. MacKAY
Music by JOHN J. HUSBAND

Joyously

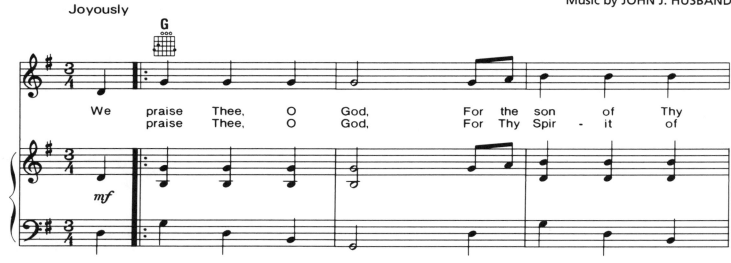

We praise Thee, O God, For the son of Thy
praise Thee, O God, For Thy Spir - it of

love, For ___ Je - sus who died, and is
light, Who has shown us who our Sav - ior, is and

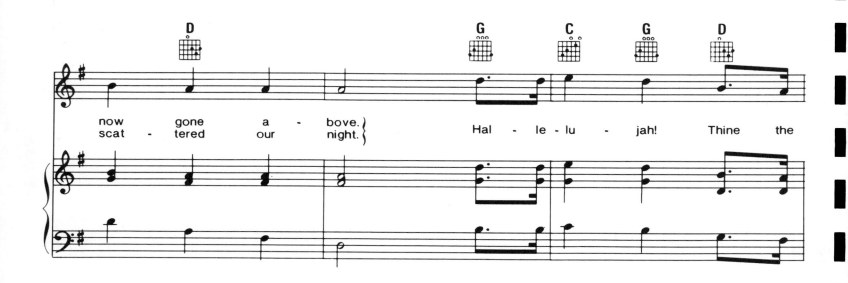

now gone a - bove. }
scat - tered our night. }

Hal - le - lu - jah! Thine the

ROCK OF AGES

Words by AUGUSTUS M. TOPLADY
Altered by THOMAS COTTERILL
Music by THOMAS HASTINGS

RING THE BELLS OF HEAVEN

Words by WILLIAM O. CUSHING
Music by GEORGE F. ROOT

1. Ring the bells of heav - en! There is joy to - day,
2. Ring the bells of heav - en! There is joy to - day,
3. Ring the bells of heav - en! Spread the feast to - day!

For a soul, re - turn - ing from the wild!
For the wan - derer now is rec - on - ciled;
An - gels swell the glad tri - um - phant strain!

See, the Fa - ther meets him out up - on the way,
Yes, a soul is res - cued from his sin - ful way,
Tell the joy - ful tid - ings, Bear it far a - way!

SAVIOR, LIKE A SHEPHERD LEAD US

Words from *Hymns For The Young*
Attributed to DOROTHY A. THRUPP
Music by WILLIAM B. BRADBURY

Quietly

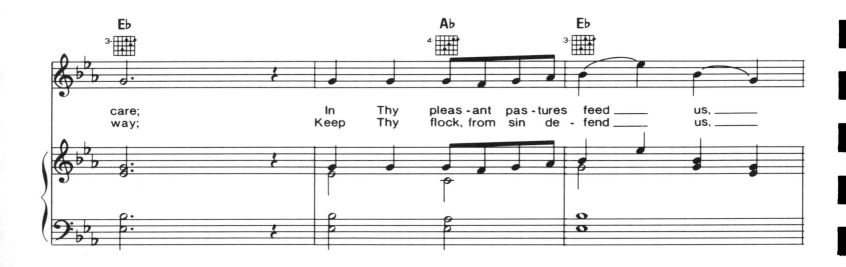

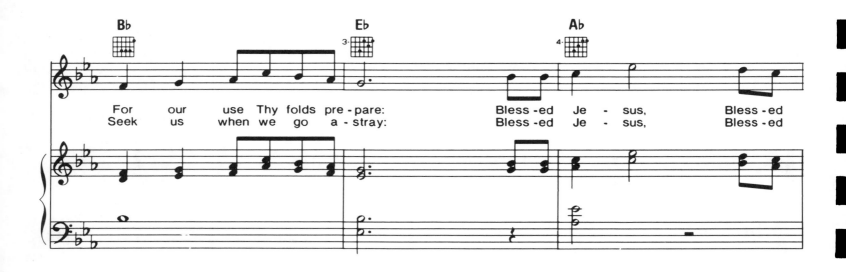

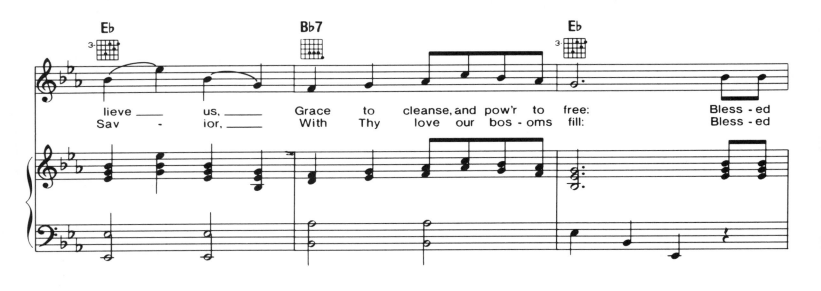

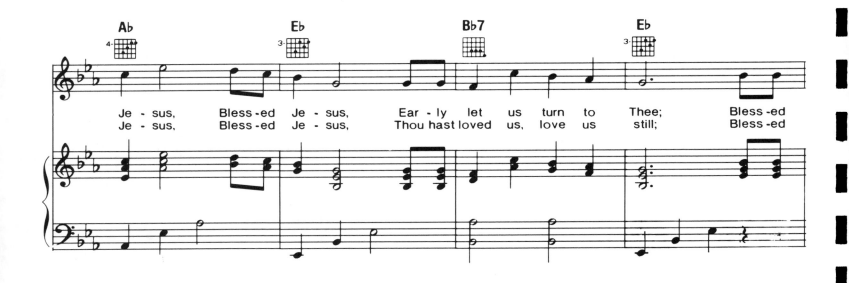

STAND UP AND BLESS THE LORD

Words and Music by JAMES MONTGOMERY
Music by CHARLES LOCKHART

SEND THE LIGHT

Words and Music by
CHARLES H. GABRIEL

Additional Verses

2. We have heard the Macedonian call today:
   Send the light! Send the light!
   And a golden off'ring at the cross we lay:
   Send the light! Send the light!
   Refrain

3. Let us pray that grace may ev'rywhere abound:
   Send the light! Send the light!
   And a Christ-like spirit ev'rywhere be found:
   Send the light! Send the light!
   Refrain

4. Let us not grow weary in the work of love:
   Send the light! Send the light!
   Let us gather jewels for a crown above:
   Send the light! Send the light!
   Refrain

SHALL WE GATHER AT THE RIVER?

Words and Music by
ROBERT LOWRY

Shall we gath-er at the riv - er, Where bright an - gel feet have

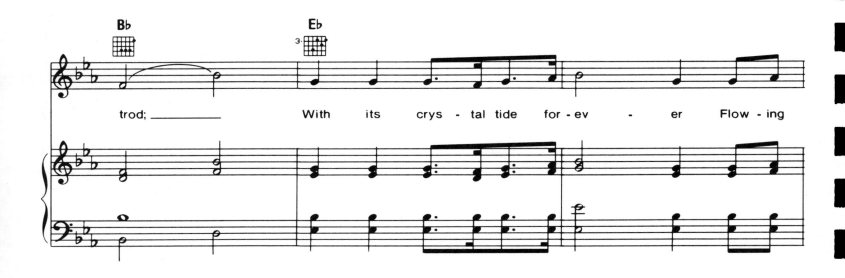

trod; _____ With its crys - tal tide for-ev - er Flow-ing

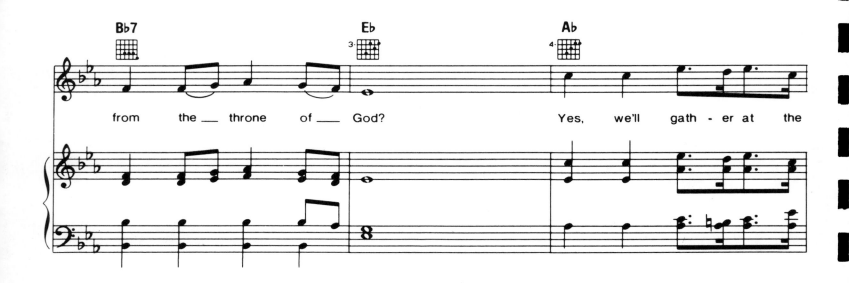

from the __ throne of __ God? Yes, we'll gath - er at the

river, The beau-ti-ful, the beau-ti-ful ___ riv - er,

Gath-er with the saints at the riv - er, That flows from the throne of __ God.

2. On the margin of the river,
   Washing up its silver spray,
   We shall walk and worship ever
   All the happy, golden day.

3. On the bosom of the river,
   Where the Saviour King we own,
   We shall meet and sorrow never
   'Neath the glory of the throne.

4. Ere we reach the shining river,
   Lay we ev'ry burden down:
   Grace our spirits will deliver,
   And provide a robe and crown.

5. Soon we'll reach the shining river,
   Soon our pilgrimage will cease;
   Soon our happy hearts will quiver
   With the melody of peace.

SIMPLE GIFTS

Traditional Shaker Hymn

SINCE JESUS CAME INTO MY HEART

Words by RUFUS H. McDANIEL
Music by CHARLES H. GABRIEL

1. What a won-der-ful change in my life has been wrought Since Je-sus came in-to my heart! I have light in my soul for which long I had sought, Since

2. sessed of a hope that is stead-fast and sure, Since Je-sus came in-to my heart! And no dark clouds of doubt now my path-way ob-scure, Since

3.,4. *(See additional verses)*

Additional Verses

3. There's a light in the valley of death now for me,
   Since Jesus came into my heart!
   And the gates of the city beyond I can see,
   Since Jesus came into my heart!
   Refrain

4. I shall go there to dwell in that city, I know,
   Since Jesus came into my heart!
   And I'm happy, so happy, as onward I go,
   Since Jesus came into my heart!
   Refrain

SOFTLY AND TENDERLY

Words and Music by
WILL L. THOMPSON

Moderately Slow

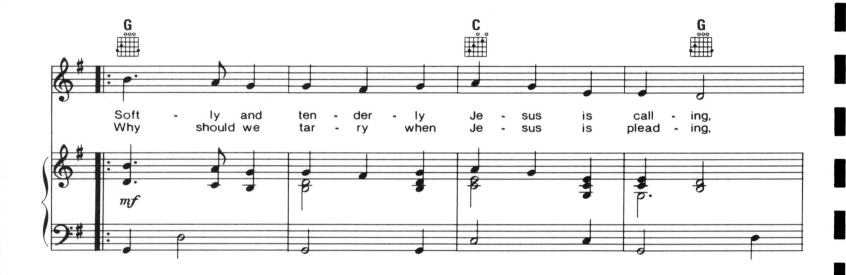

Soft - ly and ten - der - ly Je - sus is call - ing,
Why should we tar - ry when Je - sus is plead - ing,

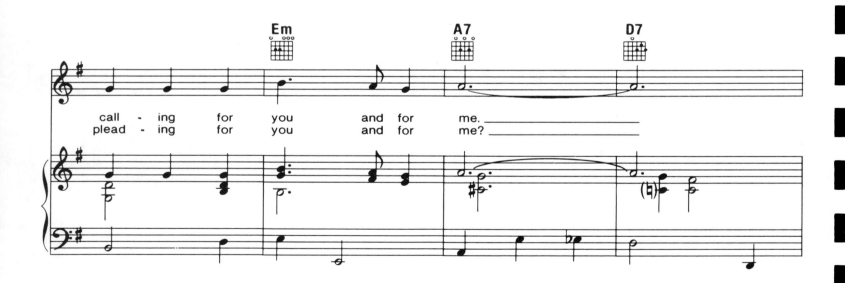

call - ing for you and for me.
plead - ing for you and for me?

SOMEBODY'S KNOCKIN' AT YOUR DOOR

African-American Spiritual

SOON AH WILL BE DONE

African-American Spiritual

Soon ah will be done - ah with the trou - ble of the world, the trou - ble of the world, ___ the trou - ble of ___ the world.

Soon ah will be done - ah with the trou - ble of the world. Goin' home to live with

SPIRIT OF GOD, DESCEND UPON MY HEART

Words by GEORGE CROLY
Music by FREDERICK COOK ATKINSON

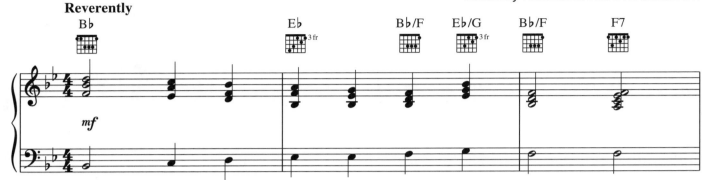

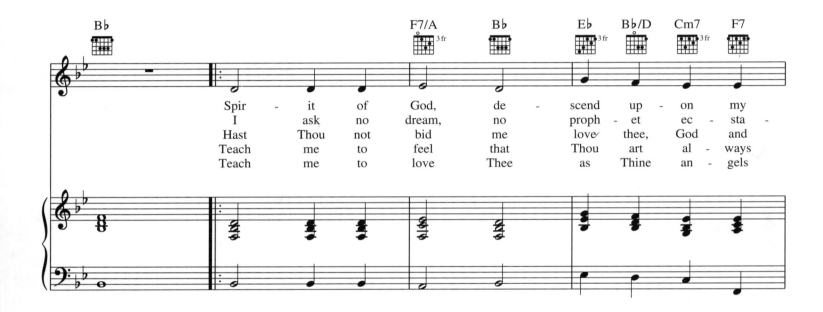

Spir - it of God, de - scend up - on my
I ask no dream, no proph - et ec - sta -
Hast Thou not bid me love thee, God and
Teach me to feel that Thou art al - ways
Teach me to love that Thee as Thine an - gels

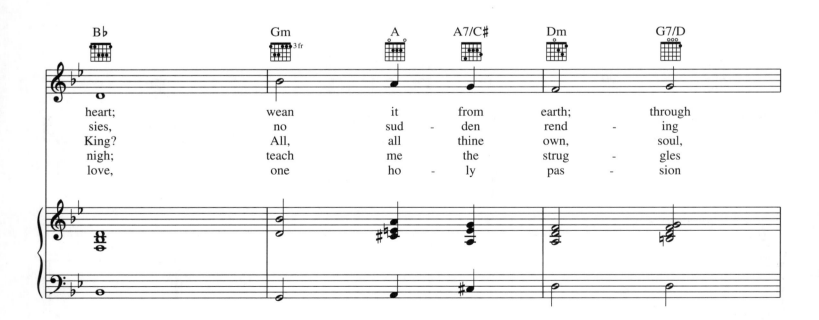

heart; wean it from earth; through
sies, no sud - den rend - ing
King? All, all thine own, soul,
nigh; teach me the strug - gles
love, one ho - ly pas - sion

STAND UP, STAND UP FOR JESUS

Words by GEORGE DUFFIELD, JR.
Music by GEORGE J. WEBB

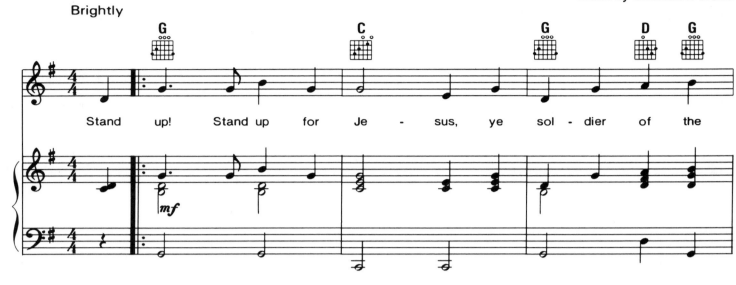

Stand up! Stand up for Je - sus, ye sol - dier of the

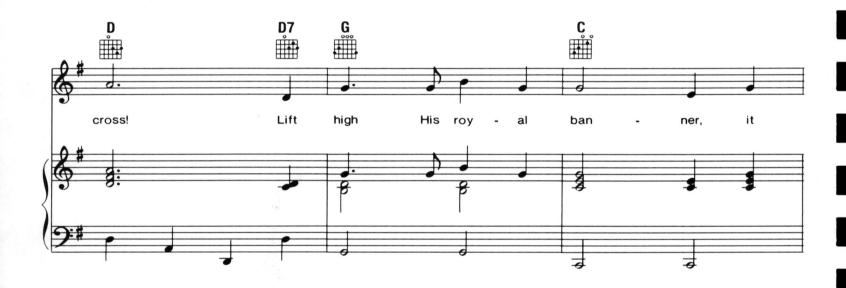

cross! Lift high His roy - al ban - ner, it

must not suf - fer loss. From vic - t'ry un - to

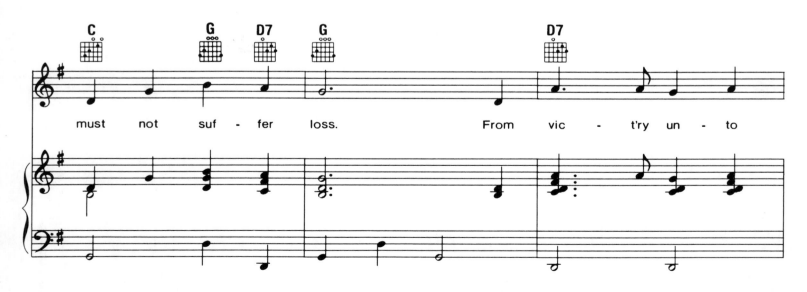

vic - t'ry His ar - my shall He lead, _____ Till ev - 'ry foe is

van - quished and Christ is Lord in - deed. Stand ly.

2. Stand up, stand up for Jesus,
The strife will not be long;
This day the noise of battle,
The next, the victor's song;
To him the overcometh,
A crown of life shall be;
He with the King of glory
Shall reign eternally.

STANDIN' IN THE NEED OF PRAYER

African-American Spiritual

STANDING ON THE PROMISES

Words and Music by
R. KELSO CARTER

1. Stand-ing on the prom-is-es of
2.-4. *(See additional verses)*

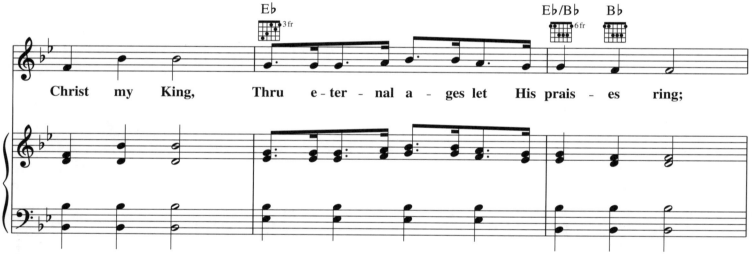

Christ my King, Thru e-ter-nal a-ges let His prais-es ring;

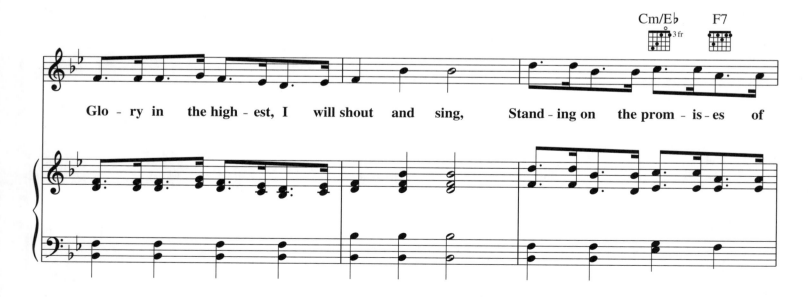

Glo-ry in the high-est, I will shout and sing, Stand-ing on the prom-is-es of

Additional Verses

2. Standing on the promises that cannot fail,
When the howling storms of doubt and fear assail,
By the living word of God I shall prevail,
Standing on the promises of God.
Refrain

3. Standing on the promises of Christ the Lord,
Bound to Him eternally by love's strong cord,
Overcoming daily with the Spirit's sword,
Standing on the promises of God.
Refrain

4. Standing on the promises I cannot fall,
Listening ev'ry moment to the Spirit's call,
Resting in my Savior as my all in all,
Standing on the promises of God.
Refrain

STEAL AWAY

Traditional Spiritual

SWEET BY AND BY

Words by SANFORD FILLMORE BENNETT
Music by JOSEPH P. WEBSTER

Cheerfully

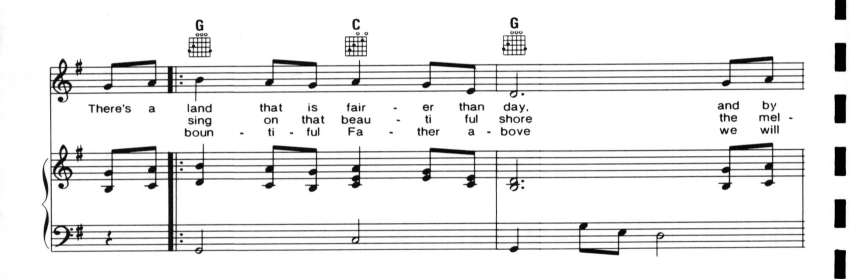

There's a land that is fair - er than day,
sing on that beau - ti - ful shore
boun - ti - ful Fa - ther a - bove

and by
the mel-
we will

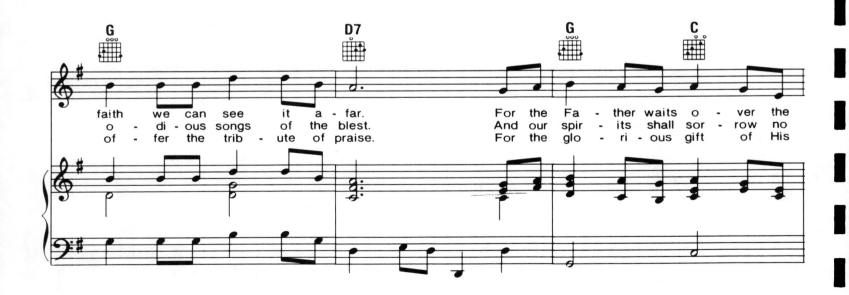

faith we can see it a - far.
o - di - ous songs of the blest.
of - fer the trib - ute of praise.

For the Fa - ther waits o - ver the
And our spir - its shall sor - row no
For the glo - ri - ous gift of His

SWEET HOUR OF PRAYER

Words by WILLIAM W. WALFORD
Music by WILLIAM B. BRADBURY

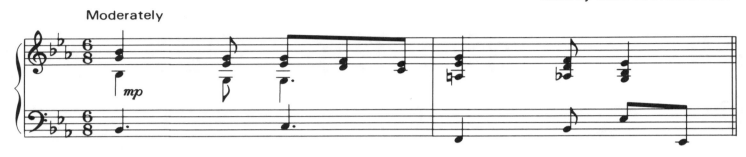

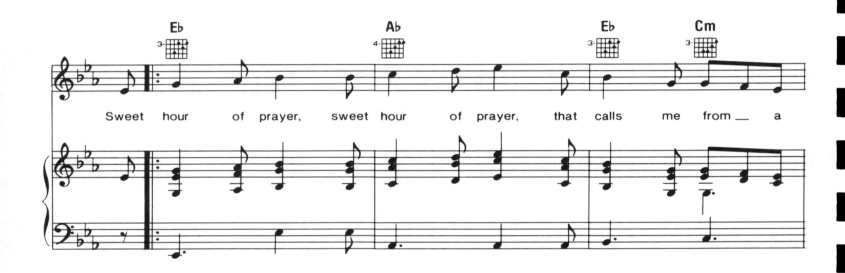

Sweet hour of prayer, sweet hour of prayer, that calls me from __ a

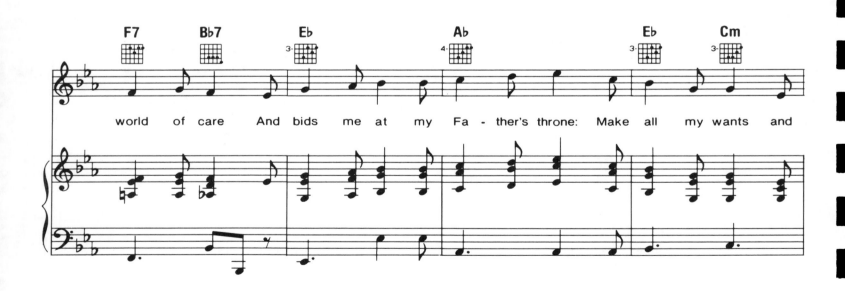

world of care And bids me at my Fa - ther's throne: Make all my wants and

2. (Sweet) hour of prayer,
Sweet hour of prayer,
thy wings shall my petition bear
To Him whose truth and faithfulness
engage the waiting soul to bless.
And since He bids me seek His face,
believe His word, and trust His grace,
I'll cast on Him my ev'ry care
and wait for thee, sweet hour of prayer.

3. (Sweet) hour of prayer,
sweet hour of prayer,
may I thy consolation share
Till from Mount Pisgah's lofty height
I view my home and take my flight.
This robe of flesh I'll drop and rise
to seize the everlasting prize
And shout while passing through the air
farewell, farewell[1], sweet hour of prayer.

TAKE MY LIFE AND LET IT BE

Words by FRANCES R. HAVERGAL
Music by LOUIS J.F. HÉROLD
Arranged by GEORGE KINGSLEY

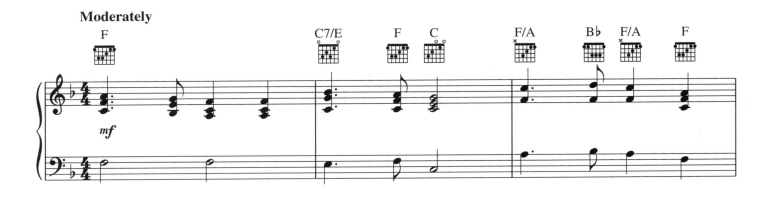

Take my life, and let it be
Take my voice, and let me sing
Take my will and make it Thine;

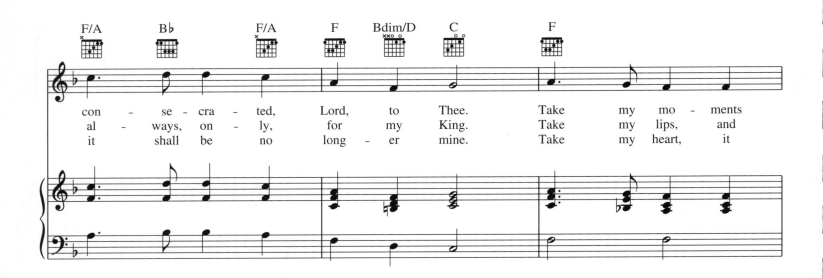

con - se - cra - ted, Lord, to Thee. Take my mo - ments
al - ways, on - ly, for my King. Take my lips, and
it shall be no long - er mine. Take my heart, it

TAKE THE NAME OF JESUS WITH YOU

Words by LYDIA BAXTER
Music by WILLIAM H. DOANE

TAKE TIME TO BE HOLY

Words by WILLIAM D. LONGSTAFF
Music by GEORGE C. STEBBINS

8vb

TELL IT TO JESUS

Words by JEREMIAH E. RANKIN
Music by EDMUND S. LORENZ

1. Are you wear - y, are you heav - y - heart - ed?
2. Do the tears flow down your cheeks un - bid - den?
3., 4. *(See additional verses)*

Tell it to Je - sus, Tell it to Je - sus; Are you griev - ing
Tell it ti Je - sus, Tell it to Je - sus; Have you sins that

o - ver joys de - part - ed? Tell it to Je - sus a - lone.
to men's eyes are hid - den? Tell it to Je - sus a - lone.

Additional Verses

3. **Do you fear the gath'ring clouds of sorrow?**
   Tell it to Jesus, Tell it to Jesus;
   Are you anxious what shall be tomorrow?
   Tell it to Jesus alone.
   Refrain

4. **Are you troubled at the thought of dying?**
   Tell it to Jesus, Tell it to Jesus;
   For Christ's coming kingdom are you sighing?
   Tell it to Jesus alone.
   Refrain

TELL ME THE STORIES OF JESUS

Words by WILLIAM H. PARKER
Music by FREDERIC A. CHALLINOR

THIS IS MY FATHER'S WORLD

Words by MALTBIE D. BABCOCK
Music by FRANKLIN L. SHEPPARD

TELL ME THE STORY OF JESUS

Words by FANNY J. CROSBY
Music by JOHN R. SWENEY

Tell me the sto - ry of Je - sus; Write on my heart ev - 'ry word. Tell me the sto - ry most pre - cious, Sweet - est that ev - er was heard. Tell how the an - gels in cho - rus

THERE IS A BALM IN GILEAD

African-American Spiritual

THERE IS A FOUNTAIN

Words by WILLIAM COWPER
Traditional American Melody
Arranged by LOWELL MASON

Additional Verses

2. The dying thief rejoiced to see
    That fountain in his day;
    And there may I, though vile as he,
    Wash all my sins away:...

3. Dear dying Lamb, Thy precious blood
    Shall never lose its power,
    Till all the ransomed Church of God
    Be saved, to sin no more:...

4. E'er since by faith, I saw the stream
    Thy flowing wounds supply,
    Redeeming love has been my theme,
    And shall be till I die:...

5. Then in a nobler, sweeter song,
    I'll sing Thy power to save,
    When this poor lisping, stamm'ring tongue
    Lies silent in the grave. Amen.

THERE IS POWER IN THE BLOOD

Words and Music by
LEWIS E. JONES

THINE IS THE GLORY

Words by EDMOND LOUIS BUDRY
Music by GEORGE FRIDERIC HANDEL

Victoriously

Thine is the glo - ry, ris - en, con - quering Son.
Lo! Je - sus meets us, ris - en from the tomb.
No more we doubt Thee, glo - rious Prince of life!

End - less is the vic - t'ry Thou o'er death hast won.
Lov - ing - ly He greets us, scat - ters fear and gloom.
Life is nought with - out Thee; aid us in our strife.

THIS LITTLE LIGHT OF MINE

African-American Spiritual

418

WAYFARING STRANGER

Southern American Folk Hymn

'TIS SO SWEET TO TRUST IN JESUS

Words by LOUISA M.R. STEAD
Music by WILLIAM J. KIRKPATRICK

TO GOD BE THE GLORY

Words by FANNY J. CROSBY
Music by WILLIAM H. DOANE

Moderately

To God be the
per - fect re -
things He hath

glo - ry, great things He hath done! so loved He the world that He gave us His
demp - tion, the pur - chase of blood, to ev - 'ry be - liev - er the prom - ise of
taught us, great things He hath done, and great our re - joic - ing through Je - sus the

Son, who yield - ed His life an a - tone - ment for sin, and
God; who the vil - est of - fend - er who tru - ly be - lieves, that
Son; but pur - er and high - er and great - er will be our

TRUST AND OBEY

Words by JOHN H. SAMMIS
Music by DANIEL B. TOWNER

THE UNCLOUDED DAY

Words and Music by
J.K. ALWOOD

WE ARE CLIMBING JACOB'S LADDER

Traditional Spiritual

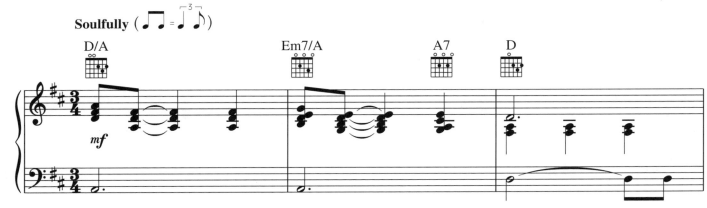

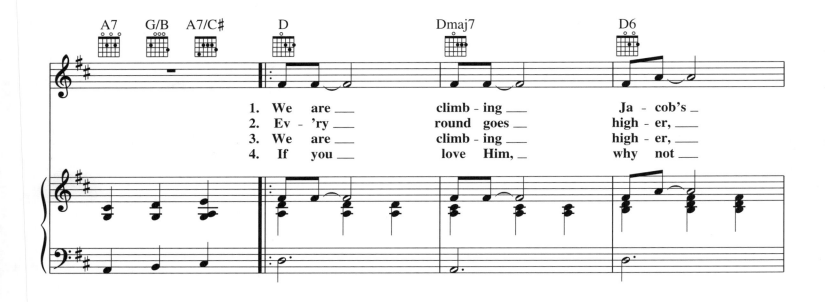

1. We are ___ climb-ing ___ Ja-cob's ___
2. Ev-'ry ___ round goes ___ high-er, ___
3. We are ___ climb-ing ___ high-er, ___
4. If you ___ love Him, ___ why not ___

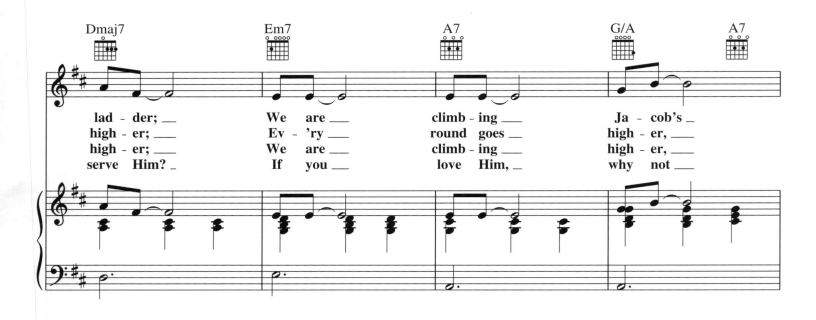

lad-der; ___ We are ___ climb-ing ___ Ja-cob's ___
high-er; ___ Ev-'ry ___ round goes ___ high-er, ___
high-er; ___ We are ___ climb-ing ___ high-er, ___
serve Him? ___ If you ___ love Him, ___ why not ___

WE GATHER TOGETHER

Netherlands Folk Hymn

WE PLOW THE FIELDS AND SCATTER

Words by MATTHIAS CLAUDIUS
Translated by JANE M. CAMPBELL
Music by JOHANN A.P. SCHULTZ

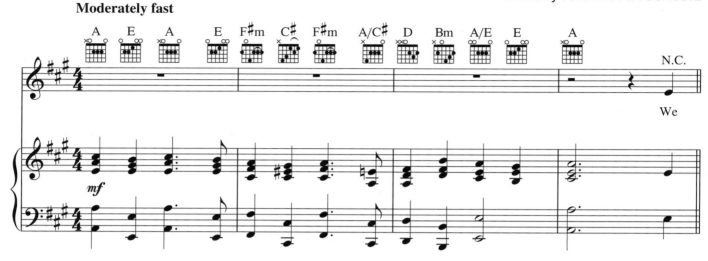

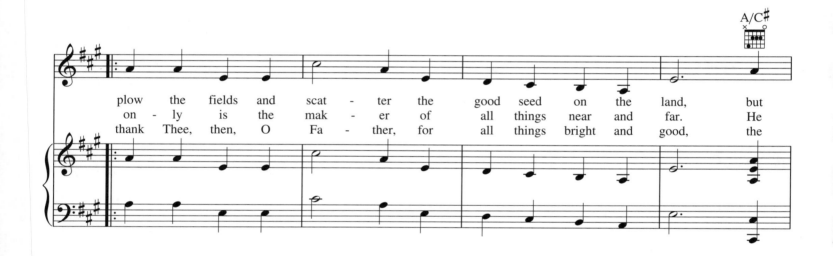

plow the fields and scat - ter the good seed on the land, but
on - ly is the mak - er of all things near and far.
thank Thee, then, O Fa - ther, for all things bright and good,

He
He
the

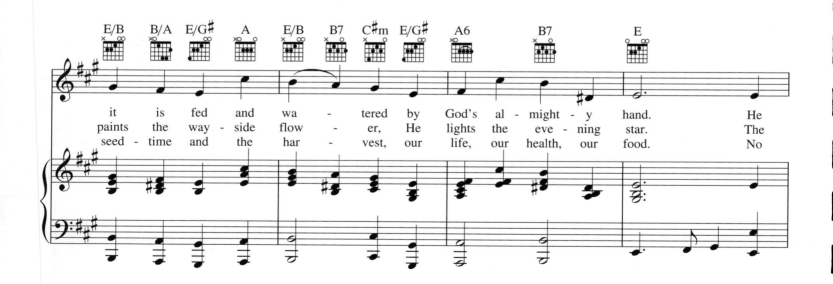

it is fed and wa - tered by God's al - might - y hand.
paints the way - side flow - er, He lights the eve - ning star.
seed - time and the har - vest, our life, our health, our food.

He
The
No

WE WOULD SEE JESUS

Words by ANNA B. WARNER
Music by FRANKLIN E. BELDEN

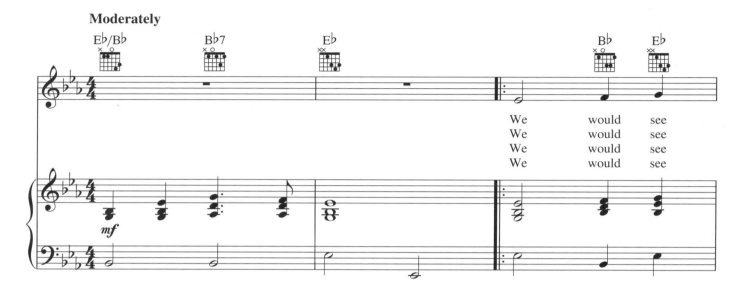

We would see
We would see
We would see
We would see

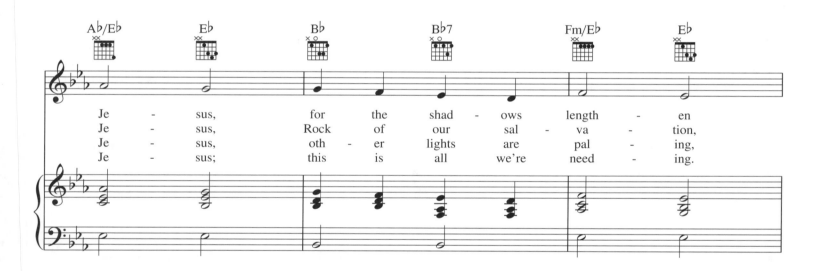

Je - sus, for the shad - ows length - en
Je - sus, Rock of our sal - va - tion,
Je - sus, oth - er lights are pal - ing,
Je - sus; this is all we're need - ing.

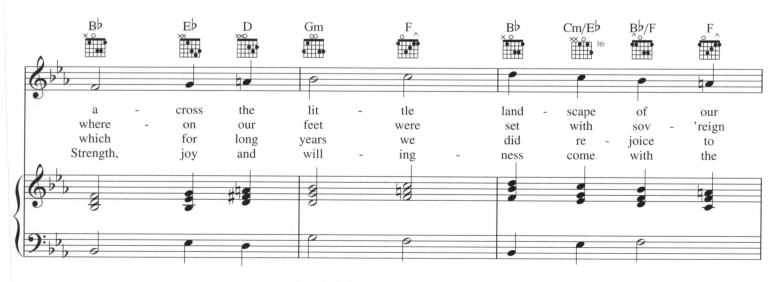

a - cross the lit - tle land - scape of our
where - on our lit feet were set with sov - 'reign
which for long years we did re - joice to
Strength, joy and will - ing - ness come with the

WE'LL UNDERSTAND IT BETTER BY AND BY

Words and Music by
CHARLES A. TINDLEY

Additional Verses

2. We are often destitute of the things that life demands,
   Want of food and want of shelter, thirsty hills and barren lands,
   We are trusting in the Lord, and according to His word,
   We will understand it better by and by.
   Refrain

3. Trials dark on every hand, and we cannot understand,
   All the ways that God would lead us to that blessed Promised Land;
   But He guides us with His eye and we'll follow till we die,
   For we'll understand it better by and by.
   Refrain

4. Temptations, hidden snares often take us unawares,
   And our hearts are made to bleed for a thoughtless word or deed,
   And we wonder why the test when we try to do our best,
   But we'll understand it better by and by.
   Refrain

WE'RE MARCHING TO ZION

Words by ISAAC WATTS and ROBERT LOWRY
Music by ROBERT LOWRY

Additional Verses

2. Let those refuse to sing
   Who never knew our God;
   But children of the heav'nly King,
   But children of the heav'nly King,
   May speak their joys abroad,
   May speak their joys abroad.
   Refrain

3. The hill of Zion yields
   A thousand sacred sweets,
   Before we reach the heav'nly fields,
   Before we reach the heav'nly fields,
   Or walk the golden streets,
   Or walk the golden streets.
   Refrain

4. Then let our songs abound,
   And ev'ry tear be dry;
   We're marching thru Immanuel's ground,
   We're marching thru Immanuel's ground,
   To fairer worlds on high,
   To fairer worlds on high.
   Refrain

WERE YOU THERE?

Traditional Spiritual
Harmony by CHARLES WINFRED DOUGLAS

Moderately

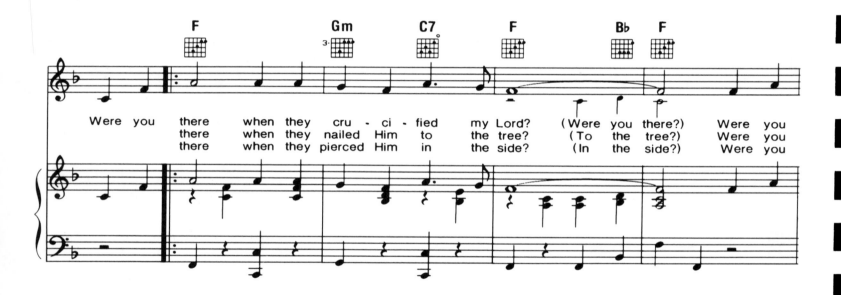

Were you there when they cru-ci-fied my Lord? (Were you there?) Were you
there when they nailed Him to the tree? (To the tree?) Were you
there when they pierced Him in the side? (In the side?) Were you

there when they cru-ci-fied my Lord? _____ Oh, ____
there when they nailed Him to the tree? _____ Oh, ____
there when they pierced Him in the side? _____ Oh, ____

WHEN THE ROLL IS CALLED UP YONDER

Words and Music by
JAMES M. BLACK

WHAT A FRIEND WE HAVE IN JESUS

Words by JOSEPH M. SCRIVEN
Music by CHARLES C. CONVERSE

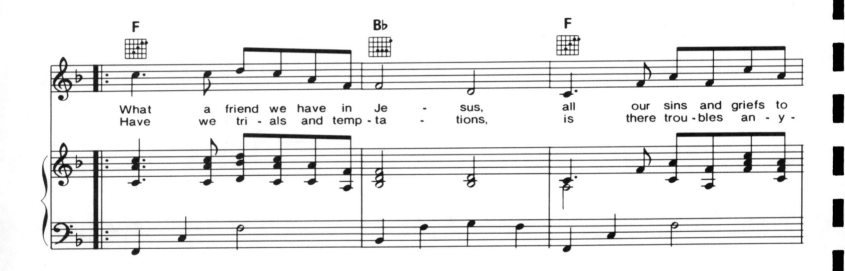

What a friend we have in Je - sus, all our sins and griefs to
Have we tri - als and temp - ta - tions, is there trou - bles an - y -

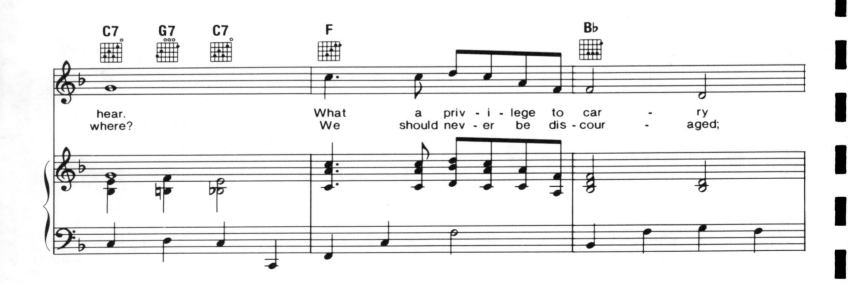

hear. What a priv - i - lege to car - ry
where? We should nev - er be dis - cour - aged;

3. Are we weak and heavy laden,
cumbered with a load of care?
Precious Savior still our refuge;
take it to the Lord in prayer.
Do thy friends despise, forsake thee?
Take it to the Lord in prayer.
In His arms He'll take and shield thee;
thou will find a solace there.

WHEN I CAN READ MY TITLE CLEAR

Words by ISAAC WATTS
Traditional American Melody
Attributed to JOSEPH C. LOWRY

WHEN I SURVEY
THE WONDROUS CROSS

Words by ISAAC WATTS
Music arranged by LOWELL MASON
Based on Plainsong

Moderately

When I survey the won- drous
For - bid it, Lord, that I should

cross On which the Prince of
boast Save in the death of

3. See, from His head, His hands, His feet,
   Sorrow and love flow mingled down
   Did e'er such love and sorrow meet
   Or thorns compose so rich a crown.

4. Were the whole realm of nature mine,
   That were a present far too small.
   Love so amazing so divine,
   Demands my soul, my life, my all.

WHEN MORNING GILDS THE SKIES

Words from *Katholisches Gesangbuch*
Translated by EDWARD CASWALL
Music by JOSEPH BARNBY

WHEN THE SAINTS GO MARCHING IN

Words by KATHERINE E. PURVIS
Music by JAMES M. BLACK

WHEN WE ALL GET TO HEAVEN

Words by ELIZA E. HEWITT
Music by EMILY D. WILSON

1. Sing the won - drous
2.-4. *(See additional verses)*

love __ of __ Je - sus; Sing His mer - cy __ and His grace.

In the man - sions, bright and bless - ed, He'll pre - pare for us a

Additional Verses

2. While we walk the pilgrim pathway,
    Clouds will overspread the sky;
    But when trav'ling days are over,
    Not a shadow, not a sigh!
    Refrain

3. Let us then be true and faithful,
    Trusting, serving ev'ryday.
    Just one glimpse of Him in glory
    Will the toils of life repay.
    Refrain

4. Onward to the prize before us!
    Soon His beauty we'll behold.
    Soon the pearly gates will open;
    We shall tread the streets of gold.
    Refrain

WHISPERING HOPE

Words and Music by
ALICE HAWTHORNE

Soft as the voice of an an - gel,
If in the dusk of the twi - light,

breath - ing a les - son un - heard. _____
dim be the re - gion a - far. _____

Hope with a
Will not the

WHITER THAN SNOW

Words by JAMES L. NICHOLSON
Music by WILLIAM G. FISCHER

1. Lord Je-sus, I long to be per-fect-ly whole; I
2.-4. (See additional verses)

want Thee for-ev-er to live in my soul, Break

down ev-ery i-dol, cast out ev-'ry foe; Now

Additional Verses

2. Lord Jesus, look down from Thy throne in the skies,
   And help me to make a complete sacrifice;
   I give up myself, and whatever I know,
   Now wash me and I shall be whiter than snow.
   Refrain

3. Lord Jesus, for this I most humbly entreat,
   I wait, blessed Lord, at Thy crucified feet;
   By faith, for my cleansing I see Thy blood flow,
   Now wash me and I shall be whiter than snow.
   Refrain

4. Lord Jesus, Thou seeest I patiently wait,
   Come now, and within me a new heart create;
   To those who have sought Thee, Thou never saidst "No,"
   Now wash me and I shall be whiter than snow.
   Refrain

WILL THE CIRCLE BE UNBROKEN

Words by ADA R. HABERSHON
Music by CHARLES H. GABRIEL

WONDERFUL GRACE OF JESUS

Words and Music by
HALDOR LILLENAS

WONDERFUL PEACE

Words by W.D. CORNELL
Music by W.G. COOPER

Moderately

Far a- way in the depths of my spir- it to- night rolls a
treas- ure I have in this won- der- ful peace, bur- ied
rest- ing to- night in this won- der- ful peace, rest- ing
thinks when I rise to that Cit- y of peace, where the
soul, are you here with- out com- fort or rest, march- ing

mel- o- dy sweet- er than psalm; _____ in ce- les- tial- like
deep in the heart of my soul; _____ so se- cure that no
sweet- ly in Je- sus' con- trol; _____ for I'm kept from all
Au- thor of peace I shall see, _____ that one strain of the
down the rough path- way of time? _____ Make _ Je- sus your

strains it un- ceas- ing- ly falls o'er my soul like an in- fi- nite
pow- er can mine it a- way, while the years of e- ter- ni- ty
dan- ger by night and by day, and His glo- ry is flood- ing my
song which the ran- somed will sing, in that heav- en- ly king- dom shall
friend ere the shad- ows grow dark; oh, ac- cept this sweet peace so sub-

WONDERFUL WORDS OF LIFE

Words and Music by
PHILIP P. BLISS

WONDROUS LOVE

Southern American Folk Hymn

WORK, FOR THE NIGHT IS COMING

Words by ANNIE L. COGHILL
Music by LOWELL MASON

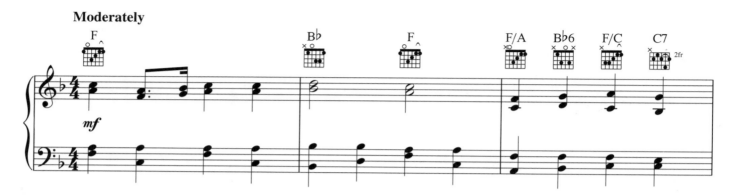

Work, for the night is com - ing,
Work, for the night is com - ing,
Work, for the night is com - ing,

work through the morn - ing hours.
work through the sun - ny noon.
un - der the sun - set skies.

Work while the dew is
Fill bright - est hours with
While their bright tints are

THE DEFINITIVE COLLECTIONS

These magnificent folios each feature a premier selection of songs. Each has outstanding piano/vocal arrangements showcased by beautiful full-color covers. Books are spiral-bound for convenience and longevity.

The Definitive Blues Collection

A massive collection of 96 blues classics. Songs include: Baby, Won't You Please Come Home • Basin Street Blues • Everyday (I Have the Blues) • Gloomy Sunday • I'm a Man • (I'm Your) Hoochie Coochie Man • Milk Cow Blues • Nobody Knows You When You're Down and Out • The Seventh Son • St. Louis Blues • The Thrill Is Gone • and more.
00311563 ....$29.95

The Definitive Broadway Collection

142 of the greatest show tunes ever compiled into one volume, including: Don't Cry for Me Argentina • Hello, Dolly! • I Dreamed a Dream • Lullaby of Broadway • Mack the Knife • Memory • Send in the Clowns • Somewhere • The Sound of Music • Sunrise, Sunset • Tomorrow • What I Did for Love • more.
00359570 ....$29.95

The Definitive Christmas Collection

An authoritative collection of 126 Christmas classics, including: Blue Christmas • The Chipmunk Song • The Christmas Song (Chestnuts Roasting) • Feliz Navidad • Frosty the Snow Man • Happy Hanukkah, My Friend • Happy Holiday • (There's No Place Like) Home for the Holidays • O Come, All Ye Faithful • Rudolph, the Red-Nosed Reindeer • Tennessee Christmas • more!
00311602 ....$29.95

The Definitive Classical Collection

129 selections of favorite classical piano pieces and instrumental and operatic literature transcribed for piano. Features music by Johann Sebastian Bach, Ludwig van Beethoven, Georges Bizet, Johannes Brahms, Frederic Chopin, Claude Debussy, George Frideric Handel, Felix Mendelssohn, Johann Pachelbel, Franz Schubert, Johann Strauss, Jr., Pyotr Il'yich Tchaikovsky, Richard Wagner, and many more!
00310772 ....$29.95

The Definitive Country Collection

A must-own collection of 101 country classics, including: Coward of the County • Crazy • Daddy Sang Bass • Forever and Ever, Amen • Friends in Low Places • God Bless the U.S.A. • Grandpa (Tell Me About the Good Old Days) • Help Me Make It Through the Night • I Was Country When Country Wasn't Cool • I'm Not Lisa • I've Come to Expect It from You • I've Cried My Last Tear for You • Luckenbach, Texas • Make the World Go Away • Mammas Don't Let Your Babies Grow Up to Be Cowboys • Okie from Muskogee • Tennessee Flat Top Box • Through the Years • Where've You Been • and many more.
00311555 ....$29.95

The Definitive Dixieland Collection

Over 70 Dixieland classics, including: Ain't Misbehavin' • Alexander's Ragtime Band • Basin Street Blues • Bill Bailey, Won't You Please Come Home? • Dinah • Do You Know What It Means to Miss New Orleans? • I Ain't Got Nobody • King Porter Stomp • Shreveport Stomp • When the Saints Go Marching In • and more.
00311575 ....$29.95

The Definitive Hymn Collection

An amazing collection of over 200 treasured hymns, including: Abide with Me • All Glory, Laud and Honor • All Things Bright and Beautiful • At the Cross • Battle Hymn of the Republic • Be Thou My Vision • Blessed Assurance • Church in the Wildwood • Higher Ground • How Firm a Foundation • In the Garden • Just As I Am • A Mighty Fortress Is Our God • Nearer, My God, to Thee • The Old Rugged Cross • Rock of Ages • Sweet By and By • Were You There? • and more.
00310773 ....$29.95

The Definitive Jazz Collection

90 of the greatest jazz songs ever. including: Ain't Misbehavin' • All the Things You Are • Birdland • Body and Soul • Girl from Ipanema • The Lady Is a Tramp • Midnight Sun • Moonlight in Vermont • Night and Day • Skylark • Stormy Weather • Sweet Georgia Brown.
00359571 ....$29.95

The Definitive Love Collection

Over 100 sentimental favorites! Includes: All I Ask of You • Can't Help Falling in Love • Endless Love • The Glory of Love • Here and Now • I've Got My Love to Keep Me Warm • Isn't It Romantic? • Love Me Tender • Save the Best for Last • So in Love • Somewhere Out There • Unforgettable • When I Fall in Love • more.
00311681 ....$29.95

The Definitive Movie Collection

A comprehensive collection of over 100 songs that set the moods for movies, including: Alfie • Beauty and the Beast • Blue Velvet • Can You Feel the Love Tonight • Easter Parade • Endless Love • Forrest Gump Suite' • Theme from Jurassic Park • One Tin Soldier • The Rainbow Connection • Someday My Prince Will Come • Under the Sea • Up Where We Belong • and more.
00311705 ....$29.95

The Definitive Rock 'n' Roll Collection

A classic collection of the best songs from the early rock 'n' roll years – 1955-1968. 95 songs, including: Barbara Ann • Chantilly Lace • Dream Lover • Duke of Earl • Earth Angel • Great Balls of Fire • Louie, Louie • Rock Around the Clock • Ruby Baby • Runaway • (Seven Little Girls) Sitting in the Back Seat • Stay • Surfin' U.S.A. • Wild Thing • Woolly Bully • and more.
00490195 ....$29.95